CREAN

THE EXTRAORDINARY LIFE OF AN IRISH HERO

Tim Foley

KEEL FOLEY PUBLISHING

Copyright © 2018, 2019 Tim Foley
First published in Great Britain in 2018 by Keel Foley Publishing
Second Edition 2019 by Keel Foley Publishing
Centenary Edition commemorating the 100th Anniversary
of Tom Crean's retirement in 1920

Title page design by Tim Foley
Front cover and chapter colour illustrations by Eglė Gostautaite.
Typesetting and interior book design by Jennifer Woodhead
Map illustrations by Thomas Bachrach
Printed in Ireland by Walsh Colour Print, Castleisland, County Kerry.

A CIP catalogue record for this publication is available from the British Library

ISBN 978-1-9999189-4-1

Keel Foley Publishing goes to every effort to ensure the use of environmentally
friendly papers that are natural, renewable and recyclable products and made
from wood grown in sustainable forests.

PRAISE FOR THIS BOOK

"Tom Crean is one of the giants of the heroic age of polar exploration and this brilliant book brings his story vividly to life and gives everyone a chance to discover a man trusted by Scott and Shackleton."

Lorraine Kelly, TV Presenter

"Absolutely amazing book about Tom Crean. Makes me proud to have Irish DNA!"

Kelsey Deanne, Actor/Film Producer

"Great book about a great Kerryman"

Timothy V Murphy, Actor

"I've been interested in polar exploration for so many years, but I really didn't know much about Tom Crean. This book is a fantastic portrait of a brilliant man and I enjoyed it so much that I immediately read it again."

Sarah Barnard, Polar Artist

In Memory of My Father

Told you I could right Dad...

Dedicated to my first grandchild, Seren Rosie

66

*We shall not cease from exploration,
and the end of all our exploring will be
to arrive where we started and know
the place for the first time*

99

T.S. Eliot

FOREWORD

Written by Julian Evans
Grandson of Admiral Edward Ratcliffe Garth Russell Evans,
1ˢᵗ Baron Mountevans

Our lives hang by a thread. For me, that thread could not have been thinner, nor more poignantly exemplified than by the heroism of just one man. In rescuing my grandfather from certain death, Tom Crean assured my very existence. So, I never tire of reading the accounts of the 'Heroic Age of Exploration' and I am always profoundly moved. I am far from alone in this respect because, as Tim Foley explains in this excellent account of his extraordinary endeavours, Tom Crean's legacy is a testament to the human spirit.

My father was introduced to Tom Crean as a babe in arms, carried to him by my, no doubt, grateful grandfather; a man whose life was not without its own stories of extraordinary courage which my family proudly celebrates. Not to say that any of us have ever been involved in similar adventures. As my late father once said, "I haven't done anything heroic in my entire life that I'm aware of."

But that's not the point. The point is we need these stories.

We need to hear them again and again because they give us reasons to strive, to endure hardships, to remember that we are fortunate to be alive.

Tom Crean is one of those human beings whose life and dee⌐ are an icon and an inspiration not just to the individual, ₧ to Ireland, but to the world. Tim Foley is right to strive national recognition for him. This account is a reminder to those of us who know and a succinct introduction to those of us who don't.

Like the Facebook page.

Wish the petition well.

Celebrate Tom Crean.

PREFACE

We all have our heroes, and the basis on which they were given that status stems from a variety of different reasons.

The subject of this book became my hero because the stories I'd heard and read about him were so incredible that I doubted such a man could ever have existed.

Interestingly, the river beside which he grew up, the *Owenascaul*, translates in English to *'the hero's river'* and the nearby lake *Loughanscaul,* similarly translates to *'the lake of the hero.'*[1] Some may see this as prophetic.

After many years of research, I learned that the stories about this man were not myths and they were witnessed and documented by his colleagues and by those who benefitted from his actions.

Although his birth was registered on 25th February in Dingle, County Kerry, church records confirm that Tom Crean was born on 16th February 1877, close to the small village of Annascaul, on the Dingle peninsula in County Kerry, Ireland. He was born at a time when the British Empire governed Ireland and many young men, seeking a way out of poverty, joined the British Navy. Among their number was Tom Crean and therein, perhaps, lies the reason his heroism has still not yet been 'officially' acknowledged by his own country.

To offer a better sense of the era, the year that 16-year-old Tom Crean joined the Royal Navy in 1893, the Second Home Rule Bill was drafted to Parliament. For a while, things looked promising for Irish Nationalists, as the Bill would have given Ireland some form of autonomy from the British Empire.

However, the Bill went the way of earlier similar proposals and was defeated in the House of Lords. It was an era when an Irish man's or woman's association with the British Empire could be seen by some as questionable due to Ireland's attempts to break free from the chains of British rule.

And, so, for Tom Crean, there has since existed a misguided belief that an impoverished, poorly educated teenager seeking a means of escape from a life of deprivation may have joined the Royal Navy out of allegiance to the British Empire. For more than a century, this belief has unjustly been a factor in how little recognition this remarkable man's deeds have received in his homeland.

The truth is actually very different. Crean, a proud Kerryman and a native Irish speaker with a fierce love for his country, entered paid service with the Royal Navy, undertaking training on depot ships, on shore establishments and out at sea. During his service, he was a member of three Antarctic expeditions over the course of a 27-year career until his retirement in 1920.

Many major historical events occurred as his career and his life, outside of naval service, progressed. Most notable among them were: the outbreak of the First World War in 1914; *the Easter Rising* of 1916; the Irish War of Independence in 1919; and the Irish Civil War in 1922. In this era of conflicts at home and abroad, Crean's heroism, understandably, went unheralded.

Crean was a dyed-in-the-wool Irishman brought up in an area where Irish was the first language. He displayed his patriotism proudly over the course of his career, nine years of which he spent seconded by the navy to serve on expeditions that took him to the most inhospitable location on the planet: Antarctica. Crean's incredible story transcends any attempts to politicise it and should be celebrated for the astonishing outcomes that allowed the very existence of the descendants of the men he saved.

Today, with a greater insight and understanding of Tom Crean's story, his case for recognition enjoys growing support regardless of a person's politics or beliefs, and I hope that one day soon the decision makers of Ireland will raise their voices in support and furnish him with the honour he richly deserves.

Until then, myself and many others are here to remind people of the remarkable story of a great Irish Hero.

ACKNOWLEDGEMENTS

Firstly, I wish to thank Julian Evans for the emotive foreword he has written. His expression of personal gratitude and his rallying call to celebrate Crean is one I'm truly grateful for.

In writing this book, I've drawn from many years of studying the life of Tom Crean and, in a digital age, it meant that not all of my detective work was undertaken on the road.

For the work that did require me travelling the country, visiting archives, and speaking to archivists, I wish to thank all those people who assisted me at the National Archives, the National Maritime Museum at Greenwich and the Royal Geographic Society (with IBG), where librarian, Julie Carrington, was particularly helpful in my search for information.

For fans of history and, in particular, naval history, there are some wonderful online resources to carry out research, and one I have to give special mention to are the naval records compiled by the late Gordon Smith whose efforts in transcribing ships' logs is an incredible piece of work. I want to also thank Andrew Martin and Phillip Martin - the use of the Irish Newspaper Archives proved invaluable in uncovering previously unknown facts about Crean's life, and I am most grateful to them for their assistance. The National Library of Australia's digital archive provided me with a wealth of information on the expeditions Crean was a member of, and I thank them for allowing me to access their great resources.

The work of oral historians Maurice and Jane O'Keefe provided me with a platform that allows first-hand accounts to be documented for future generations, and I'm thankful that Tom Crean was well remembered by those who lived alongside him.

There's a plethora of books on polar exploration that cover the expeditions that Tom Crean was a member of and, although some differ in their versions of events, all of them were helpful in my research.

The book also contains two images featuring Tom Crean that I uncovered during my research. Having searched high and low for images of Tom Crean over the years, I was thrilled to discover two newspaper clippings that featured his image. They remain in a grainy state and have been restored a little for my book but their authenticity is priceless for providing a sense of the era.

For the colour illustration of Tom on the front cover and for those that introduce the chapters covering Crean's heroics, I wish to thank the talented Eglė Gostautaite for her great skill in depicting the scenes.

It is wonderful to be able to take a visual glimpse into Tom Crean's past and, for the images of Annascaul featured in this book, I wish to thank the National Library of Ireland for permission to use the great photographs taken by Robert French that form a part of the Lawrence collection. Thanks also to Erin Carrie, who proofread the book and never tired of my adding new content.

For the illustrations in the book that have been used to depict eviction scenes in late nineteenth century Ireland, I wish to thank Richard Hickey and Maureen Costello of Mayo County Libraries for their help and assistance in providing images from the wonderful Maggie Land Blanck collection.

Maggie had been used to my requests some years back when she held the collection and I thank her also for approval of their use. Thanks, also, to Dr David Wilson who showed kindness in allowing me to use a sketch drawn by his great uncle and two-time expedition colleague of Tom Crean, Edward A. Wilson.

I also wish to acknowledge Michael Smith and his book, *An Unsung Hero, Tom Crean - Antarctic Survivor*. After reading it, I was left inspired to dig deeper into the life of my hero and after two years immersing myself in research for the book, I feel I've achieved this.

My gratitude also goes to the author and historian, Ryle Dwyer, for approval of the images of his articles about Tom Crean that appear in this book.

The Irish Genealogy website, operated by the Department of Culture, Heritage and the Gaeltacht, is a goldmine of information for anyone seeking information about their Irish roots, as were The National Archives of Ireland and the Census project. I spent many hours on both and I'm grateful they provided me the information that helped compile information on the family of Tom Crean.

For those interested in learning more about the rescue of the men on Elephant Island, the website, *patbrit.org*, created and operated by Duncan Campbell and Gladys Grace is a great resource. There, I discovered all the transcripts of the Magellan Times publication that related to Shackleton, Crean and Worsley's arrival in Punta Areas up to the time they left after carrying out the rescue. My gratitude also goes to Tansy Bishop, National Archivist at the Falkland Island's Jane Cameron Archives, who was extremely helpful while I was researching Tom Crean's time on the island in 1916.

Another great online resource was the Internet Archive; the collection of digital books and web resources they have amassed were extremely helpful to me.

I deliberately focused this book on the life and heroics of Tom Crean in the hope that it will provide a concise telling of his story. To achieve that best, I drew, in the main, upon publications and accounts written during his lifetime and predominantly written or spoken by the people he lived or served alongside. I felt that, in doing so, I could transcribe a truer perspective of the character.

There were some exceptions to this; one of them being the superb account of William Lashly's life written with great passion by George Skinner and his wife Valerie, who happens to be a descendant of Lashly.

As this section is entitled 'Acknowledgements', I want to thank all those who share my huge admiration for Tom Crean through the Facebook platforms that exist as a great online legacy. Ultimately, if we reach the goal of achieving official national recognition for Tom Crean, it will be because of those who supported the campaign on Facebook and who have signed and continue to sign the petition. I wish to also thank the journalist Tadhg Evans for his excellent coverage of the campaign in *The Kerryman* newspaper.

Over the time I've operated the campaign on Facebook, I've enjoyed great support from *Stair na hÉireann*, a wonderful web based resource on Irish History, and I wish to thank the administrator, Padraig Keane, and his cousin, Caroline Ryan, for helping to give the campaign wider exposure through their great platform.

Our petition was handed to the Irish Defence Minister, Paul Kehoe, on 7th February 2018 in Dublin by the landlady of the South Pole Inn (and huge Crean fan), Eileen Percival, and school pupil, Lea Carey, from St Mary's School in Sandyford, Dublin.

The increasing number of Tom Crean fans stretches right across the globe and, one day, I'm sure we'll enjoy the biggest ceilidh in celebration of achieving the ambition of Ireland providing official, national recognition for Tom Crean.

Please head to our Facebook page and click on the 'Like' button. It can be found at:

www.facebook.com/honourtomcrean

Tim Foley

CONTENTS

——— 66 ———

*Hardships often prepare ordinary
people for an extraordinary destiny*

——— 99 ———

C.S. Lewis

Chapter 1

THE ROAD THAT
LED SOUTH

Growing up in Salford, England, the son of a County Kerry man, I had an early introduction to the beautiful county of my father's birth. My father was born in Keel, Castlemaine, birthplace of the *Wild Colonial Boy* and an entry point to the Dingle peninsula, one of the world's most scenic routes.

As the years passed and my familiarity with Kerry grew, I became aware of a strangely named pub while travelling to visit relatives in the village of Annascaul. 'Why on earth...', I pondered, among a host of typically named Irish bars, '...would someone think to call a pub the *South Pole Inn*?' Over the years, my intrigue got the better of me and, upon reaching an age that I developed greater interest in my surroundings, the reasons became apparent. The bar was adorned with pictures on every wall of the man who named it so. He was a man whose remarkable feats of incredible bravery were legendary among the polar expedition community.

A few kilometres up the road from the pub lies the townland of Gortacurraun. In 1877, it was a community of small dwellings where families resided in cramped, cold conditions. It was in one of these small houses where farmer Patrick Crean and his wife, Catherine, would raise their family. Thomas Crean, the seventh of eleven children, was born at a time when opportunities were rare for those across an Ireland still suffering in the aftermath of the *'Great Famine' (An Gorta Mór), 1845-52*. Within three years of Crean's birth, the *'Little Famine' (An Gorta Beag) of 1879* had taken root across Ireland after successive disastrous harvests in the preceding years. By 1880, Irish emigration figures rose to more than double the previous year, as 100,000 people left their home shores in search of better fortune.[1]

Records and newspaper articles of the time paint a dismal picture of life for the poor and destitute living in late nineteenth-century Ireland. It was also a time when ruthless land agents, representing their landlord masters, were frequently carrying out evictions in a repugnant ritual replicated across the whole of Ireland. On 31st March 1880, the weekly meeting of the *Annascaul Relief Committee* sat surrounded by almost 150 men and women applicants from the area who, it was reported, *"presented a very destitute appearance."*[2]

With no possibility of growing potatoes and with no seed available to them, many had walked for miles to collect a ration of 'indian meal,' an imported corn flour used, in the main, to make bread, on which they had to survive until the next meeting. For many families, *'Poor Relief'* (assistance for the poor based on the Poor Relief (Ireland) Act 1838) was essential to help avoid a life in the workhouses. Operated by a Board of Guardians in Poor Law Union districts across Ireland, property rates levied on landowners were calculated by the Guardians and used to fund their governance. Each district had a workhouse where those in the most dire of circumstances were housed. It was a fate that many had to suffer in institutions where children, many of them orphans, were high in numbers. In February

1883, almost 1,100 people populated the workhouses of Dingle and Tralee and, of these, almost half were children under the age of fifteen.[3]

It was a hopeless time, when children of the poor had to walk barefoot. Raising a large family meant long, hard hours of working the cattle and the fields just to keep from starvation.

Fathers often called on their sons and daughters from an early age to help them with their labours and the Crean household was no exception.

With poor sanitation, families were at grave risk from diseases and there was little they could do to improve the circumstances of their hand-to-mouth existence.

Farmers relied on the good health of cattle and, in the cold of winter, often brought them into their dwellings where animals also provided a valuable heat source to the occupants. To build or erect a shed in which to house animals, meant an increase in rent; so, rather than face even greater penalties, they unwittingly placed themselves in peril from infections from the livestock they owned.

To compound the misery, Annascaul families faced further dangers as fresh water supplies were scarce. Water taken from the river or wells presented yet another risk of disease.

In stark contrast, for the landowners and visiting British gentry, Annascaul and the Dingle Peninsula had a wealth of fishing and hunting grounds, all of which were reserved for their exclusive enjoyment.

Attracted by the magnificent surroundings, and its wildlife, a host of poets, artists, botanists and naturalists ventured into the imposing hillsides and beautiful beaches that encircle the village in search of inspiration or their next scientific discovery. In the days

William O'Brien, Irish Nationalist politician and journalist. Making a case for a Navy training ship to be sited in Cork, his home county:-

Correspondence to the First Lord Of The Admiralty.

"If it be admitted that Ireland is entitled to at least one training ship, then I think the claim of Cork Harbour to be selected as its station is beyond any reasonable dispute, by two facts. First, that Queenstown is the Irish Headquarters of the Royal Navy and, second, that of 220 boys joining the Navy from Ireland last year (1892), 97, or considerably more than a third of the whole, came from Cork."

Irish Examiner, 26th August, 1893

His request and that of other Irish representatives conveying concerns of worried parents witnessing their sons travelling long distances to English ports, was listened to but never acted upon.

when the class system divided the haves from the have-nots, life's leisures and luxuries were being lived out amidst the squalor and suffering of the poor.

At the age of twelve, Tom Crean's school days at the nearby Brackluin school ended, and his father summoned him to begin his working life on the farm.

The beauty of the surrounding coastal landscape was of little consolation for the contrasting misfortunes of impoverished farm life in nineteenth-century Ireland. A number of sons and daughters felt that, to change their fortune, they must emigrate to another land and many took this route to seek a better life.

Those who were fortunate enough to find paid work in their adopted homelands would send money home to help their families pay the rent. Eviction was a constant threat to those who fell into arrears, unable to pay the extortionate rents levied upon them by landlords.

Groups of men employed by the land agent (the landlord's representative) accompanied by police - the *Crowbar Brigades*, as they were known across Ireland - would ruthlessly force their way into a property that had, more often than not, been barricaded by the fearful tenants. On entry, they would eject the homeowners from their property while the police and sympathetic neighbours looked on.

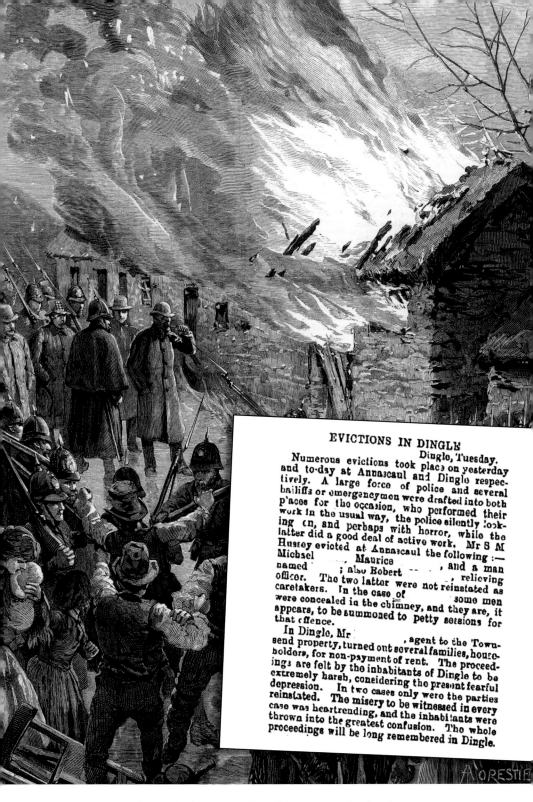

EVICTIONS IN DINGLE

Dingle, Tuesday.

Numerous evictions took place on yesterday and to-day at Annascaul and Dingle respectively. A large force of police and several bailiffs or emergencymen were drafted into both places for the occasion, who performed their work in the usual way, the police silently looking on, and perhaps with horror, while the latter did a good deal of active work. Mr S M Hussey evicted at Annascaul the following :— Michael ____, Maurice ____, and a man named ____ ; also Robert ____, relieving officer. The two latter were not reinstated as caretakers. In the case of ____ some men were concealed in the chimney, and they are, it appears, to be summoned to petty sessions for that offence.

In Dingle, Mr ____, agent to the Townsend property, turned out several families, householders, for non-payment of rent. The proceedings are felt by the inhabitants of Dingle to be extremely harsh, considering the present fearful depression. In two cases only were the parties reinstated. The misery to be witnessed in every case was heartrending, and the inhabitants were thrown into the greatest confusion. The whole proceedings will be long remembered in Dingle.

Typical eviction scene in 19th century Ireland

CLOCKWISE FROM LEFT: A view of Annascaul showing the single storey dwellings to the left of the bridge where Tom Crean would, in 1929, build The South Pole Inn • An evicted tenant family • The track from Crean's birthplace at Gortacurraun into Annascaual Village • HMS Impregnable, the ship in which Tom Crean was trained for a life at sea.

In February 1886, a total of twelve families, amounting to over fifty men, women and children, were evicted from their Annascaul homes by gangs operating under the stewardship of the infamous land agent Samuel Hussey.[4] It was a dark backdrop in the formative years of the young Tom Crean, who may well have gazed out across the horizon of the coastline that surrounded him and wondered what lay beyond the hardships and sufferings to which he was bearing witness.

With seven brothers and three sisters, prospects for the young Tom Crean looked bleak unless he were to take control of his own destiny.

That opportunity arose in 1893. After a series of petty arguments with his father, the latest seeing him take the blame for allowing cattle to stray into a potato field,[5] young Tom Crean made a decision that would alter the course of his life. Like many young Irishmen of his era, Tom Crean decided to join the Royal Navy. Many of his acquaintances from neighbouring areas joined up in the months and years before and after him and, in 1893, no fewer than fifteen boys from Annascaul, Ventry, Ballinacourty, Minard, Lispole and Dingle travelled the same path to a new life.[6]

Joining the Royal Navy was, surprisingly, a route that was found acceptable in an area that was a hotbed of rebellion against the Crown.[7] The belief that naval recruits were unlikely to meet fellow countrymen in the field of conflict may have played a part in this this as would the fact that those recruited as ratings were not required to swear an oath of allegiance to the Crown.[8] Signing up to the navy was, therefore, a longstanding and traditional means of escaping poverty for the sons of Annascaul.[9]

No matter that he was just 16 years old, he made his way to Minard, a short distance from his home, where the British Navy coastguard station was located. Upon receiving his papers, Tom Crean's new life in the Royal Navy as a Boy 2nd class, began on 10th July 1893.

Crean's service record signifies that he was born on 20th July 1877,[10] and it was not until 2015 that a genealogist, Kay Caball, discovered his birth certificate dated 25th February 1877.[11] His true date of birth however, 16th February 1877, albeit under a different christian name, can be found in the parish registers of the period and I've elaborated on this in the Appendix. Incorrect birthdates are anomalies that exist in many of the birthdates listed for a number of naval recruits of the time; yet, the reasons, if any, remain unclear.

After undertaking a medical at Dr John Moriarty's in Dingle, Crean headed down to Queenstown, (now Cobh), by train.

Accompanying him was a local acquaintance from Minard, James Ashe. Already a 10-year navy veteran, Ashe was travelling back to HMS Victory 1, the shore-based holding barracks at Portsmouth, after a period of leave.[12] James was a relation of Thomas Ashe, the Irish martyr and patriot who later, in 1917, died after being force-fed during a hunger strike at Mountjoy prison.

In Queenstown, James, who was fond of a drink or two, stopped by a local bar. Outside,

Royal Navy

'There are vacancies in the Training Ships for Boys from 15 to 16½ years old, of good character, able to read and write, physically fit for service and up to standard, viz:-

AGE	HEIGHT	CHEST
15 - 15½	5ft.0in	31
15½ - 16	5ft.1½	30½
16 - 16½	5ft.2½	31½

Pamphlets containing information as to conditions of entry, pay and prospects, etc., can be obtained at any post office. For further information, apply by letter to one of the following officers:- Captain H.M.S. Impregnable, Devonport; the Officer of any Coastguard Station...'

The Guardian,
31st December, 1892

11

waiting to board the boat to England, Tom Crean became embroiled in a scuffle with another boy. Separated by an RIC constable, it was only after showing his newly signed naval documents to the officer, that he was allowed to board the boat.[13]

One imagines it would have been heartbreaking for Crean leaving his family and the magnificent shores of the Dingle Peninsula; yet, a life beyond the horizon was one he seemed destined for.

HMS Impregnable, the depot ship to which he was first assigned, was a training ship based in Devonport where Crean was one of over 1,500 boys living in a cramped environment below deck.[14] Conditions onboard drew such cause for concern over the health and wellbeing of the boy recruits that questions were being raised in the British parliament.[15] Concerns were heightened when the death toll aboard *Impregnable* had reached alarming rates in comparison to other training establishments.

Life as a boy recruit in the navy was only for the hardiest and discipline was extreme. Boys would rise at 5:00 a.m., carry their hammocks to the upper decks for storage before they would thoroughly scrub the decks, polish the ship's brasses and the utensils in the mess decks until they were shining spotlessly.

Punishments were severe and were carried out without compunction for even the most minor of offences. If, during the daily inspection call, a boy was seen to have a button missing or his uniform was not spotlessly clean, his instructor would note it and, should it reoccur, he would receive six swipes of the cane. A harsher and more public punishment awaited those who were caught smoking or those arriving back late from shore-leave. All crew would assemble on the quarterdecks, the offender would then be brought midships where he was tied arms and legs to a wooden horse before the ship's corporal dished out twelve strokes of a stout cane, each end covered with wax-string and reversed every four strokes. The most severe punishment was meted out to those who had been insolent to an instructor or had been caught stealing. Again, the offender would be tied to the wooden horse and twenty-four lashes of the birch would strike his bare-skinned body. The horrific spectacle would have served as a warning, not only to the poor victim but to the boys who witnessed it.[16]

In this harsh environment, dreams of a better life must have seemed as distant as ever for young Tom Crean and it would be safe to assume that he would have had regrets about his decision to join up.

Crean, though, was raised from hard Kerry stock and he soon matured into adulthood. Developing a strong character was essential at a time when no-nonsense taskmasters ran their crews under strict navy protocol.

Crean's early training consisted of general schooling and seamanship carried out aboard the training ship. Gunnery training was undertaken on the drill fields of nearby shore bases. As time progressed, all boys had to be ready to go to sea and, for this, training brigs attached to the mother ship were used. Daily forays over a course of twelve weeks, from the brig that boys were assigned to, would ensure they became accustomed to undertaking their duties out at sea.[17]

Throughout his training schedule on various ships and training establishments, Crean would cross paths with others from his locality who had signed up before or after him. The familiar sounds of home, where even the Irish officers conversed in their native tongue while relaxing or playing cards in the officer's mess, must have provided him some comfort in the uncomfortable surroundings he found himself in.[18]

When he left *HMS Impregnable* to join *HMS Devastation*, the Port guard ship at Devonport, in November 1894, Crean's rating had changed to Boy 1st Class.

After a voyage that took him across the Atlantic and after joining the crew of *HMS Wild Swan* in December 1894, Crean was transferred to *HMS Royal Arthur* in March 1895. During his service aboard, his progression through the ratings saw him reach Ordinary Seaman, an automatic rise in status for those reaching their 18th birthday and for boys who had, in the eyes of the Royal Navy, become men.

Aboard *HMS Royal Arthur*, the flagship assigned to the Pacific Station in South America, Crean was a member of a crew that included William Lashly.[19] It is likely they became familiar with one another and the two men would not only be thrust into playing a part in a major international incident, they would later share in an historic tale of a very different kind and in a very different place.

It was during Crean's service aboard *HMS Royal Arthur* that he was first called to action, as the ship, along with *HMS Wild Swan* and *HMS Satellite*, entered the port of Corinto, in Nicaragua, on the morning of Tuesday 23rd April 1895.[20]

Operating under the command of Rear Admiral Henry Stephenson, the small naval task force was on a mission to collect compensation of £15,000 (almost £2 million in today's currency) from the Nicaraguan government. In late 1894, the Nicaraguans had occupied the Mosquito Coast, a disputed territory spanning the coastlines of Nicaragua and Honduras and the natives looked to Britain for protection.

The arrival of the three ships at Corinto was sparked by the seizure of the British Vice Consulate at Bluefields, the largest town on the disputed territory, where Nicaraguan forces had arrested some twenty British subjects and confined them in the Nicaraguan capital, Managua.

Commander Stokes of the *Royal Arthur* left the ship and handed over an ultimatum to the Nicaraguan Minister for Foreign

Affairs. Admiral Stephenson's demands, contained in a letter and a proclamation, allowed the Nicaraguans three days to meet the conditions and to hand over the payment. Failure to do so would see the town of Corinto occupied by a landing force and other Nicaraguan ports blockaded.

After the deadline for handover of the indemnity passed on 27th April 1895, a detachment of 400 men from the naval force occupied the town without opposition and Martial Law was declared. Captain Frederick Trench, commander of *Royal Arthur*, was installed as the new Governor as the British flag was raised over Customs House.

Further escalation loomed large, as the Nicaraguans sought protection from the USA for what they considered an illegal invasion of their territory but the Nicaraguan President, José Santos Zelaya's, overtures to his American neighbour were resisted with the US proclaiming: *"We decline to protect a wrongdoer in her wrongdoings."*[21]

Now directing their response from Managua, the Nicaraguan government boycotted the port and ceased all supply lines and provisions in an effort to isolate the British forces. After a tense stand-off, with Nicaraguan forces having retreated outside of the town, negotiations began and eventually, on 3rd May, an agreement, helped forward by the offices of the USA, was reached to pay the amount and agree to the conditions of the ultimatum.

With the crisis at an end, the ships headed out of Corinto on 5th May 1895; yet, not without further incident, as Captain Trench had, during his short-lived governance of the town, contracted a fatal bout of gastritis while ashore. As the ships set a course for Esquimalt in British Columbia, Canada, Trench was buried at sea.[22]

Crean's first outing as an Ordinary Seaman had thrust him into the last throes of an ailing empire flexing its muscles and had brought him close to armed conflict thousands of miles beyond the horizon of his beloved Kerry. For the young Irish sailor, his first active assignment turned out to be a baptism of fire he would hardly have imagined when leaving home two years earlier.

He transferred once again to *HMS Wild Swan* (in October 1895) and his rating rose to that of an Able Seaman. By 1st June 1898, Crean was made Leading Seaman serving at the naval barracks, *HMS Vivid,* at Devonport. From this point in his career, a topsy-turvy navigation up and down the ranks ensued. After postings to the Devonport-based gunnery school depot ship, *HMS Cambridge*, and *HMS Defiance*, the navy's Torpedo and Submarine Mining School at Plymouth, he was downgraded to Able Seaman and upgraded to Petty Officer 2nd Class within the space of a year, in 1899.

It's understandable that the initial years of Crean's navy life had left him with great cause for doubting his decision to join up. Never would he have imagined that the strict punishments meted out to boy recruits and the potential for armed conflict would play any part in his fledgling career. It was, by any standards, a rude awakening for the young Tom Crean.

For the following two years, Crean would serve on a number of shore establishments and training ships that increased his arsenal of naval skills.

While stationed in New Zealand aboard *HMS Ringarooma* from 15th February 1900, twenty-three-year-old Crean would, again, be demoted to Able Seaman. The reasons for what must have been a miserable six-year period in his life are unclear but naval regulations would downgrade a rating for the slightest misdemeanour and Crean, like most young men, enjoyed his share of grog and a smoke of his pipe. Unfortunately, naval protocol rendered the slightest of transgressions onboard ship punishable and demotions were a frequent part of that process. Returning late from shore-leave or caught smoking or drinking outside of designated periods would be deemed sufficient reasons for demotion and it's not rare to see similar instances on other naval records of the time.

Serving aboard *Ringarooma,* Tom Crean's life would unexpectedly take another turn - one that would lead him to a place that would become his second home: Antarctica.

Robert F. Scott was a naval officer with big ambitions and his ship, *RRS Discovery*, undergoing repairs, was dry-docked in Lyttelton, New Zealand, soon to embark on a mission to explore the undiscovered continent. The ship had been built in Dundee for the purpose of the expedition but, on the voyage to New Zealand, she had displayed a vulnerability to leaks which required urgent attention before the expedition got underway.

During the journey from England, the officers of *Discovery* had a hard time controlling an unruly nucleus among the crew who had been identified as bad influences, particularly while under the consumption of alcohol. Shore-leave at stop-off ports was a time for the crew to relax and, more often than not, that equated to seeking the nearest bars in search of a few drinks. Problems occurred when a number of the men returned to duty aboard ship a little worse for wear and, on occasion, there would be altercations with shipmates. It was one such incident, while the ship was berthed at Lyttelton, that led to Commander Scott's recruitment of Tom Crean.

Having a record already littered with time in the cells for insubordination, one of the crew, Able Seaman Henry John Baker from Folkestone, Kent, England[23], who Scott recalled had returned to the ship drunk while it was moored at the previous port of Cape Town, almost came to blows[24] with Thomas Kennar, a petty officer. The drunken sailor had continued to maintain his reputation for indiscipline and, indifferent to a severe reprimand from Scott, he fled the ship on 6th December 1901.[25] His expedition was at an end. On 10th December 1901, now a deckhand short, Scott recruited Crean from *HMS Ring-arooma* for the journey south and it's entirely possible that Crean's abilities were recommended to Scott by members of *Discovery* he had previously served alongside, among them Kennar and William Lashly, who had served with Crean during the Corinto incident.

Incidentally, for Baker, the cells again beckoned. Over a year later, he was recovered from desertion on 17th February 1902 and charged for being absent without leave and using insulting language to a superior officer.[26]

On board the *Discovery* were a host of crew members making the same pioneering journey to the southern continent, men with whom Tom Crean would form lifelong bonds. Among them were Ernest Shackleton, William Lashly, Frank Wild, Edward Wilson and Edgar 'Taff' Evans, a Welsh powerhouse of similar stature to Crean and a man from a similarly impoverished background.

Discovery set sail on 21st December 1901 and, as she made her way out of Lyttelton to the cheers of onlookers onshore and a flotilla of boats either side, a young sailor, giddy with the excitement of it all, climbed to the top of the main mast to get a better view. Standing near the crow's nest, (the lookout platform at the top of a ship's main mast), he waved back to the crowds on the steamers that were accompanying *Discovery* out of the harbour, when the rope he was holding onto gave way.

He fell 120ft head-first to the deck, where his head struck an iron reel. 23-year-old Able Seaman Charles Thomas Bonner of Stepney, London, died almost instantly.[27]

Discovery, with its ensign flying half-mast and with *Ringarooma* alongside, sailed into Port Chalmers where Bonner's body was placed into a coffin. It was then mounted upon a gun carriage and, after a funeral with military honours, he was buried in the local cemetery.[28]

It was a sad start to Tom Crean's first journey to Antarctica, the place he's become most associated with.

On his maiden expedition, Crean was, for a period in early June 1902, incapacitated due to severe swelling of his legs and, for a time, it was thought he had contracted scurvy, the disease that was the scourge of explorers of the age. His weight dropped by twenty pounds over the course of the month, however, the 'dropsical' symptoms he displayed were identified more recently as most likely being oedema and he made a full recovery.[29]

A good, early indication of Crean's powers of resilience were evident in a short summary of the expedition's work from March 1903, in a letter written by Scott to the Royal Geographic Society dated March 23rd 1904 in which he stated:

"Lieut. Barne left the ship on September 12th, placed a depot to the south and returned on September 20th. His party included Lieut. Matlock, Quartly, Smith, Crean and Joyce. They experienced the lowest temperature for a sledging party on record, the thermometer remaining almost continuously below -60 degrees and registering so low as -68 degrees. Under these very severe conditions, there was only one very severe frostbite. This was one of Joyce's feet, which, on two occasions, had to be nursed back to life for more than an hour."

A reminder, if any were needed, of the dangers of working in the unknown, treacherous landscape of Antarctica came when one of

Crean's expedition colleagues plunged to his death.[30]

As blizzard conditions erupted during a sledging mission to place dispatches and to establish a cairn at Cape Crozier, and with poor visibility making further progress almost impossible, a decision was made for the majority of the party to return to the ship. Three men - Lieutenant Royds, Reginald Koetlizz the expedition doctor, and Reginald Skelton - continued on to Cape Crozier with a lighter load.

The returning party of nine men encountered worsening temperatures and blizzard conditions when ascending a range of hills relatively close to *Discovery*. On reaching the summit, conditions became impossible and they pitched their tents.

Nourishment for explorers in the colder climes of Antarctica came in the form of hoosh, the recipe being made up of a dried meat and fat concoction (Pemmican), mixed together with sledging biscuits and hot water. Rations of hoosh provided nutrition and helped energise weary bodies on their long-haul missions. On this occasion, owing to a broken Primus stove, the men were forced to eat cold Pemmican which one of the party likened to *"eating sawdust."*

In danger of freezing to death in their tents, they decided to let the dogs loose, abandon their sledges and make a dash for the ship.

The sloping surface outside was like glass and a heavy mist allowed them only a few inches of visibility. Two men - George Vince and Clarence Hare - had left the tent wearing fur boots. It was a short-sighted decision as they slipped and slid aimlessly across the ice. Hare decided to leave the group and attempt a return through the thick fog back to the tent to retrieve more suitable footwear. It was a foolhardy decision and, when he had not returned, the men formed a chain and set off in a futile attempt to find him.

As they travelled further, the slippery surface became almost impossible for them to navigate across and one of the men, Edgar Evans, stumbled and shot out of sight down a slope.

Lieutenant Barne, the leader of the group, immediately followed him down to make rescue but he too disappeared, followed by a third man.

The remaining five, unable to find their fallen colleagues decided to continue pressing on in a desperate bid to reach the ship. Vince, in his fur boots, was holding on to Frank Wild, the only man wearing spikes, when suddenly he let go and slid out of sight appearing to fall over a sharp edge.

It was only as the party met with clearing conditions and soft snow that they realised they had been skirting an overhanging cliff 200ft above the sea below. The sad fate of Able Seaman George Vince of Blandford, Dorset, now dawned upon them.

Clarence Hare's fate met with better fortune after he had become exhausted when searching for the tent. Astonishingly, after 46 hours missing and with two search parties on successive nights unable to locate him, he nonchalantly strolled towards the ship to the amazement of the crew observing the shuffling figure approaching them. Among those watching were Evans and Barne who had made it back to the safety of the ship.

Ironically, it was the blizzard that appeared to have been his saviour, as the snow drift had covered him as he lay sleeping.

How he survived was beyond all logic but, incredibly, he suffered no ill effects and stated *"It was a wonderful experience, but I don't want another of the same sort."*[31]

In what was officially hailed as a mission of great scientific importance, the aptly named *Discovery* expedition also provided invaluable lessons for subsequent missions to Antarctica. Scott later admitted that *"food, clothing, everything was wrong, the whole system was bad."*

It was also an expedition on which more than one Irishman was leaving his stamp on Antarctica. Dublin-born Hartley Ferrar's geological work unearthed fossils that provided evidence of a supercontinent existing 320 million years ago connecting Antarctica to: Africa, South America, Australia, the Arabian Peninsula and the Indian subcontinent. Ferrar also became the first person to locate the presence of coal seams in the Prince Albert mountains of Victoria Land.

It all proved fitting that another emblem of the Irish presence in Antarctica, an Irish ensign, flew proudly on the back of Tom Crean's sledge.

Discovery was also famed as the expedition that laid down the marker for future attempts to break the records for reaching farthest south; yet, it was also noted for being the one that was to divide two leaders - Shackleton and Scott - who were to play a major role in Tom Crean's career.

Shackleton had been returned home by his commander, Scott, after taking ill while attempting the record. It was a decision Shackleton found hard to bear and his relationship with Scott was to sour from the moment he was ordered home. Left scarred from Scott's orders, Shackleton later decided to go it alone. After raising private funding, he returned to Antarctica aboard *Nimrod* in 1907 to attempt the ultimate goal of reaching the South Pole itself. It was a goal that evaded him but he did achieve the coveted record of reaching the farthest south.

The story of *Discovery* could easily have ended similarly to that of one of its successors, the *Endurance,* a decade later, when the frozen ice held her locked in its jaws.

On its return to the expedition in January 1904, having unloaded provisions for the expedition in the previous year, the *Morning*, *Discovery*'s relief ship, was accompanied by another vessel, *Terra Nova*.[32] It would later become the ship upon which Scott would make his last and fateful journey to Antarctica.

Seeing the two ships approach shattered Scott's plans for extending his stay to a third winter and he was left bitterly disappointed at what he considered a premature ending of his exploration endeavours.

To make matters worse, the *Morning's* skipper, Captain William Colbeck, carried with him orders for Scott to abandon *Discovery* if she could not be freed from the ice. With just a six-week window before all three ships would be in danger of becoming icebound, the crews set about the task of freeing *Discovery*. Sawing operations had already begun to open up a path to the sea back in 1903 and, yet, it had proved soul-destroying for the crew who made little progress as they worked in four-hour shifts with little time for rest in between. It was a futile task in which even the saws became frozen in the ice.

Neither the crew nor officers wanted to suffer the indignity of returning to England carrying news of their pioneering discoveries aboard two relief ships. It had become a matter of pride and a renewed concerted effort began with the crews of all three ships combining to help rescue *Discovery* from the ice that imprisoned her.

During the operations to release the ship, Tom Crean's career could so easily have come to an abrupt end on his maiden expedition but for the life-saving efforts of two of his crewmates: petty officers William Smythe and David Allan.

In February 1904, Crean, who was to become the lifesaver extraordinaire, was working by *Discovery* for his part of the efforts to free her from the ice, when a crack opened up and he fell into the sea.

CUTTING OUT THE DISCOVERY FROM THE ICE.

The officers of the Terra Nova, on the arrival of that vessel at Plymouth, gave a correspondent of the "Daily News" some particulars of the work of the relief ships sent to the aid of the National Antarctic Expedition. After the Morning and the Terra Nova sighted the Discovery on January 8 Captain Scott paid them a visit, covering the twenty miles of ice behind which lay the Discovery by means of sledges. The crews of the Morning and the Terra Nova prepared to blast the ice, with a view to cutting out the imprisoned ship. Hopes, however, were very low, for the Discovery was twelve miles further in the ice than when the Morning had communicated with her in the previous year. Spaces about 12ft. square were blasted at a time, and the pack, aided by the easing due to the season, began soon to break away. The men often worked until midnight, and, after having turned in for an hour or two, would be called out again to make another start at the outer edge of the ice, which was about 6ft. thick. On February 14, owing to a fierce blizzard, the blasting operations were very considerably hindered, the men working under the greatest difficulty. But still they laboured heroically on, and that afternoon they had the satisfaction of knowing that the channel had been cut to within two miles of the Discovery.

The ice then began to break up freely, and by night the relief vessels were no more than a quarter of a mile from where the Discovery was lying. The crew of the Terra Nova then tried the old whalers' dodge of rolling the ship with all hands, and at a quarter past ten that night the Terra Nova was alongside the Discovery. Next day the latter was free, yet so certain had the officials been that she would be permanently entombed in the ice that they had taken the precaution of transferring all the gear and instruments, as well as the records of the Discovery's sojourn in the ice, to the relief ships. Indeed to such an extent were these preparations advanced that the crew of the Discovery were apportioned equally to the Morning and to the Terra Nova, notices to that effect being posted up on the Discovery. Those allotted to the Morning were to have left on February 27, whilst the Terra Nova was to have sailed a week later for home. The Terra Nova supplied the Discovery with coal, after which the homeward voyage was entered upon.

The Guardian 17th August 1904

LIEUTENANT ARMITAGE AT THE GRAMMAR SCHOOL.

Through the kindness of Mr. Burditt, of Heaton Chapel, the boys of the Grammar School had a delightful hour yesterday afternoon listening to an account of the English Antarctic Expedition given by Lieutenant Armitage, who was second in command on the Discovery. The lecturer was able to show no fewer than 140 slides, nearly all of them taken during the expedition, the only exceptions being a few from the Jackson-Harmsworth quarters in Franz Josef Land, which were made use of to draw contrasts between North and South Polar experiences. Not the least interesting of these was a photograph of a white Siberian dog, one of whose descendants, a pet of Lieutenant Armitage, was the only dumb animal that lived through the three years spent by the ship in southern latitudes. Not only were the pictures new to those who had already had the advantage of hearing Captain Scott, but for the most part the incidents by which the story was enlivened were new also. Occasionally the lecturer raised some interesting problem which he left to the boys to solve. Does the great sheet of ice, for example, of which Ross's Barrier is the northern edge, stretch right across the South Pole to Weddell Sea, or does it only run into a bay of which Victoria Land and King Edward VII.'s Land are the extreme ends? "I am often asked," the lecturer said, "if the South Pole will ever be reached. My answer is that it would be well to make the attempt over the Barrier with such animals as these (throwing on a screen a picture of a pair of Siberian ponies), which we found so invaluable in the Jackson-Harmsworth Expedition." Among the photographs shown were some taken by Lieutenant Armitage illustrating the changes taking place in the glaciation of these regions. In one respect Lieutenant Armitage thought the arrangements in Franz Josef Land were better. He thought it was much healthier for the men to live in a hut than on board the ship. Lieutenant Armitage concluded with a word or two about the kindness shown to the crew by the people of New Zealand. "Two of the officers are already married to New Zealand ladies, four more are engaged, and a number of the seamen have followed suit. Indeed they were very kind."

In introducing the lecturer Mr. Paton said he once had an ambition to go to the North Pole himself, but he had found his way to Long Millgate instead. He asked the boys to show by their cheers how proud they were of men like Lieutenant Armitage. This was done.

The Guardian
27th January 1905

He was hauled out of the icy depths; yet, typical of his character, he carried on with his task regardless that his own life had been in the balance. No sooner had he returned to his duties than he fell in again and had to be rescued a second time.[33] A litany of falls into ice crevasses and freezing waters were documented throughout the course of Tom Crean's Antarctic career and it's a wonder that he survived them all.

When all hopes to free the ship appeared lost, unexpectedly better weather came to the rescue and the ice began to fragment. With the additional use of dynamite to blow open a channel, the ship was finally able to navigate a way out of the ice.

It had been a close call and a permanent stay of execution for the ship that today welcomes visitors descending on its Dundee home where it has become a major maritime attraction.

After returning from the *Discovery* expedition, Crean returned to duty at the shore-based navy barracks *HMS Pembroke* at Chatham, during which time he was rewarded with a promotion to Petty Officer 1st Class on 10th September 1904, thanks to the recommendation of Scott. His upgrade in naval status was notable as being the most significant upgrade of the returning crew members and was a reflection of his growing reputation as a highly valued member of the expedition.

Upon his return, the navy that Crean had joined some eleven years earlier was undergoing wholesale change under the stewardship of Admiral John Fisher. Fisher's reforms were considered revolutionary for the period as he quickly set about modernising the navy and its 'Man O' Wars' (battleships). *HMS Dreadnought* would set the standard in terms of speed and strength and, after its completion in 1906, a whole suite of new ships in her class became known as the 'Dreadnoughts.' These heavily armoured giants, and those built by other nations in response, would meet at the cost of thousands of lives in the First World War eight years later. For Crean, it is hard to imagine a man whose reputation would be that of saving lives having to serve out a career doing the polar opposite.

Tom Crean's naval career had also changed and the 16-year-old boy who had served a hard, unhappy apprenticeship, had evolved into a polar explorer with a growing reputation. As if to rubber-stamp the transition from his first steps aboard the training ship and the harsh naval discipline he had been subject to, he was now attending Receptions and Award ceremonies in recognition of his contribution to the pioneering exploration of Antarctica.

On 13th September 1904, along with his *Discovery* colleagues, he walked through a large crowd who had assembled outside of Portsmouth's Town Hall,[34] anxious to catch a glimpse of the returning explorers who were to be entertained at a dinner in honour of their achievements. At the Civic reception given by the Lord Mayor and attended by a host of dignitaries and naval hierarchy, Scott, shortly after a promotion to the rank of Captain, told his audience:

"It had been three years since the expedition had left the neighbourhood and they had been very eventful and busy years for us. We had had time to think of our homecoming but I do not think that, in our wildest dreams, the members of the crew would have conceived that we would be received in the manner we had been received. It was particularly gratifying to us to have the reception at Portsmouth and I would like to explain to the Mayor that all appreciated his feast but we could imagine how much more it would have been appreciated in Antarctic regions, if we had had it served up on the great barrier or on the inland ice."

It was at Portsmouth where Lieutenant Michael Barne presented Crean with a Royal Geographic Society silver medal award for his service on the *Discovery* expedition.

In the years before the dramatic events of two subsequent British Antarctic expeditions that would grab worldwide attention, Tom Crean was now a member of an exclusive group who the public viewed with ever-increasing admiration.

On 1st October 1904, Crean had resumed naval duties and remained in Portsmouth serving at the torpedo school, *HMS Vernon*. At the Royal Albert Hall on 7th November 1904, with a vast audience in attendance, the remainder of the officers and crew of *Discovery*, were presented with their silver medals by the Royal Geographic Society in recognition of the pioneering work they'd undertaken.[35] Although unable to attend the ceremony, Crean's contribution to the expedition would, no doubt, be remembered and recalled by those present.

Commenting about the medal recipients, the man considered to be the godfather of exploration, RGS president Sir Clements Markham, in an early description of Crean stated:

"An excellent man, tall with a nose like Lord Hood, always willing, always cheerful, universally liked. He received a free discharge on his return: but re-joined."[36]

In another comment, made in his biographical dictionary of the *Discovery* expedition, Markham's comments revealed that Crean's thoughts remained close to his home and loved ones at a time when his fortunes had changed yet theirs had remained the same.

"Crean Thomas, Able seaman aged 26. He joined the 'Discovery' from the 'Ringarooma' at Port Chalmers in Dec 1901. Pay

£55.14.11 a year. He allots to his mother Mrs K Crean, Annascaul,
Co. Kerry. A good man. Got a free discharge, but came back to
the service."[37]

Crean, whose 12 year naval service engagement would have
ended on 20th July 1907, was being offered an early discharge but
it is unsurprising he was keen to remain in the Navy where he now
felt content and valued for his services. His annual pay, equivalent to
£7,000 in today's currency, helped keep his family safe at a time when
the distress and evictions of the poor in Ireland remained as high as
when he'd left Kerry 12 years earlier.

Confusingly, there is a third quote attributed to Markham that
signified Crean's mother Catherine had died whilst he was serving on
Discovery. Markham is quoted as saying:

"An excellent man, tall with a profile like the Duke of Wellington,
universally liked. He received a free discharge as his mother had
died: but he thought better of it, and came back to the Navy."[38]

Catherine was, in fact, very much alive and would live another 20
years before her passing. Quite why Markham would state this is puz-
zling. The 75-year-old Markham was at the end of his own tenure as the
RGS president and it is possible he was referring to another expedition
member. If he was not, then he had clearly been misinformed.

For Tom Crean, the reception he and his colleagues received
after the return of *Discovery*, would not be the last time the unas-
suming Irishman would be present at similar events at exclusive
venues. Given his humble nature, it is hard to imagine how a man
reared in impoverished surroundings and hewn in the harshest of
environments, dealt with being thrust into the glamour and applause
of such occasions.

Serving as effectively as he had on *Discovery* had earned him high praise from his commanders, which subsequently resulted in a climb through the ratings and an increased pay packet.

It was an outcome that would not have been lost on Crean and further promotions would help realise his ambitions back home in Ireland when his period of engagement was up.

Further shore-based assignments on successive training establishments, *HMS Vernon* at Portsmouth and *HMS Ganges* in Suffolk, followed before his return to *HMS Pembroke* until September 1906.

During this period and while on leave, Crean made trips home to Annascaul and it's an interesting thought to imagine Crean lamenting upon the beauty of his homeland to colleagues. If so, his musings certainly rubbed off on Dr Edward Wilson, the junior surgeon and zoologist who he served with on the *Discovery* expedition.

For the whole of August 1905, the Wilson family took up residence at Sketchers Cottage facing the magnificent Inch Beach just a short distance from Annascaul. While there, Wilson, a talented artist, drew a number of sketches of the surroundings including some of Crean's village.[39] Today, a number of the drawings are housed in the County Kerry Museum and it's possible that Crean encouraged and influenced Wilson to make the trip.

1906 might have been a year that saw Tom Crean take part in his second expedition to Antarctica but the plans of Lieutenant Michael Barne to lead the next British Antarctic Expedition never quite materialised.[40] If they had, then Crean, whose sledge-hauling skills Barne had been very familiar with after serving together on *Discovery*, would, it's safe to assume, have been high on his list of recruits.

On 18th September 1906, when Tom Crean joined the crew of *HMS Victorious* between further attachments to *HMS Pembroke* at

Chatham, it was the first of four postings alongside Captain Scott: on *HMS Albemarle* (1907), *HMS Essex* (1908), and *HMS Bulwark* (1909).

While serving on *HMS Essex* with Scott, Crean received the sad news that his eldest brother, Hugh, had died at the Gortacurraun home after a bout of pneumonia.[41] Hugh's widow, Johanna, was left with the task of bringing up their seven children while helping to tend to the farm.

Through the grief, Tom Crean's life in the navy continued and it's a great testament to his abilities that Scott clearly held him in such high regard to request that he serve alongside him. On 3rd April, Crean was attached to *HMS Actaeon*, the torpedo school at Sheerness before returning to *HMS Pembroke* on 9th September 1909. It was to be his last posting before being entered on the ledger of *HMS President*, the shore-based stone frigate used as an accounting base for sailors who were assigned elsewhere. Crean's 'elsewhere' was to be his second expedition to Antarctica.

In the to-and-fro quest for 'Southern Glory', the next attempt to reach the Pole fell to Scott and Crean was one of the first people in whom he confided. It appears also that the passage of time had healed Scott's relationship with Shackleton seven years after returning him home from the *Discovery* expedition. Evidence of this was provided in an article by the esteemed political journalist, Sir Henry Lucy, who, writing in March 1913 after the world first learned of Scott's fate, said:

"The last time I saw Scott was in the first week of June 1910. Looking in on Shackleton at his office in Regent St, I found the two Antarctic heroes in close consultation about the forthcoming expedition (Terra Nova).

Antarctic Expedition

'The crew of the *Terra Nova*, which left yesterday for the South Pole, were subject to anthropological experiments with a view to determining what effect the frigid environment of the South Pole will produce on the skin pigments of explorers. It remains to be seen whether the Antarctic chill will bleach their hairs or change the colour of their eyes and skin. The crew's hair, features and hands were looked at with a tintoscope and the colours jotted down in the case of each individual for comparison with their appearance on their return from Southern seas. A good many of the crew, it is interesting to note, are Irishmen from the Western counties.'

Irish Independent, 2nd June, 1910

In conversation with his friends, Shackleton made no secret of his dominating desire to make a second dash to the South Pole, feeling assured that, this time, he would reach it. It was characteristic of the feeling between these two men that, whilst Scott had generously devoted himself to assisting Shackleton in preparation for his expedition (Nimrod), Shackleton scrupulously stood aside whilst Scott made his second attempt, with equal zest and devotedness, giving his old commander the benefit of his experience and advice."[42]

The *Terra Nova* expedition set forth from Cardiff on 15th June 1910 and onboard with Crean were a number of polar veterans including Edward Wilson, William Lashly and his friend Edgar Evans. Scott's second in command was another Evans, Lieutenant Teddy Evans. The name 'Evans' would become one forever associated with Tom Crean.

Making their first voyage to Antarctica were three men from Crean's neighbouring county of Cork which was well represented on an expedition that included: Patrick Keohane from Courtmacsherry, Robert Forde from Cobh, and a skilled helmsman, Mortimer McCarthy, from Kinsale.

32

The *Terra Nova* expedition entered the annals of history as Scott's attempt to become the first man to reach the South Pole. It was a failed attempt that saw the final team lose both the race and their lives. It did, though, win the hearts and minds of the public, becoming the stuff of legend. Understandably, this story overshadowed that of others and, in particular, the story of heroism surrounding Tom Crean.

The following four tales are accounts of the life-saving feats of Tom Crean over the course of two of the expeditions he made to Antarctica between 1910 and 1916.

———— **"** ————

*Courage is an instinct seldom
denied by the truly brave*

———— **"** ————

Leif Tomy

Chapter 2

TOM
THE JUMPER

For a short while on his first expedition to Antarctica, on board the *Discovery,* Tom Crean was a member of the sledging team that held the prized 'Farthest South' record. On 11th November 1902, Crean was part of a depot-laying group under the command of Lieutenant Michael Barne. The record was achieved when they passed the 78°50'S latitude previously reached by the Norwegian explorer, Carsten Borchgrevink, on 16th February 1900.[1] It was a short-lived achievement because, just over a month later, his Captain (Robert F. Scott), Ernest Shackleton and Edward Wilson extended the record to 82°11'S. The expedition, the main purpose of which was to survey a largely undiscovered continent, helped pave the way for the challenges of future expeditions including the ultimate accolade of reaching 90°S (The South Pole).

While serving on *Discovery,* Crean cemented his reputation as an invaluable powerhouse whose stamina and strength were great attributes in a landscape and climate that demanded no less. The impression he made on Scott was evident and, in the years after *Discovery* returned to Britain in 1904, Tom Crean would accompany Scott on all four of his seagoing naval postings prior to the race for the South Pole.

The *Terra Nova* expedition (1910-1913) would see Scott's attempt to be the first to reach the South Pole. It was during this, Crean's second expedition under Scott's command, that his heroics were first called upon.

In the early hours of 1st March 1911, while hauling a six-week supply of food, oil and equipment on a return journey to the expedition's base at *Hut Point*, Crean, along with Henry Bowers and Apsley Cherry-Garrard, encountered fierce blizzards that hampered their progress.

With four heavy sledges and four of the expedition's ponies (in an emaciated state, as a result of the long journey and conditions), reaching their destination as soon as they could was of paramount importance.

Bowers, the group's leader, had orders to follow the dogs whose tracks would guide them back to their base. It soon became apparent that dogs, unlike their human counterparts, did not comply to the orders of their masters and they set off wildly and without direction. They quickly became invisible in the mist of the blizzard that was enveloping the three men.

Left without the ability to follow tracks, the party continued their march and their journey back would take them over sea ice. With additional orders, dispensed earlier by Scott, they were to set up camp only if weather conditions rendered it absolutely necessary.

Visibly, there was little to distinguish safe ice underfoot from thinner ice and, as they continued their journey, cracks were becoming more frequent and water was oozing from between the cracks. It had become a journey fraught with danger. Had the dogs travelled a path over the same sea ice back to Hut Point, it would have been of little use following them, given the far greater weight of the party and their sledges. In any event, dog tracks would not be visible on the ice.

Guiding the ponies and with the four heavy sledges in tow,

Bowers made a decision to turn back. Making matters worse, a black mist had descended and the ponies were suffering from exhaustion, stopping frequently. It became a matter of urgency to find safe ground on which to rest and they eventually reached a snow-covered area that appeared to be a good place to set up camp.

After building ice walls to protect the ponies from the elements, they fed the animals, hurriedly pitched their tent and crawled inside to take shelter from the weather and prepare some hot food.

With a faulty Primus stove that took one-and-a-half hours to boil a kettle of water, the three men dined on a ration of hoosh.

After finishing their meal, Bowers (a Lieutenant), supplemented their energy ration with a hot cup of cocoa and, in the darkness of the tent, he mistook a bag of curry powder for their chocolate treat. Still unaware of his mistake, he stirred some sugar into a cup and handed the first to Crean who downed it in one before realising what it was. There is no record of Crean's reaction but one imagines it being gulped down without being noticed, providing him a much-appreciated heat source at the time.

At 2:00 p.m., the men took to their sleeping bags and very soon fell asleep. It was two-and-a-half hours later when Bowers awoke suddenly to a noise. Assuming it was the snores of his still-sleeping companions, he was about to lay his head back down when he heard a loud crack. He rushed out of the tent to discover that their camp was now sitting on a floating mass of broken ice. In his panic, he had failed to put on his Finnesko boots and had taken to the ice wearing his socks.

Already one of the four ponies had fallen victim to the sea below and, so, their urgent fight for survival had begun. Two of the sledges carrying vital supplies were perilously close to the edge of an adjacent floe. Calling out to his colleagues, Bowers managed to pull the sledges onto the thirty-yard diameter floe on which they had now become stranded. As he did, their floe split into two. Fortunately, they remained together on one piece, but the situation by now was looking dire.

It became clear that the men were not merely intent on saving themselves but also saving the supplies and the three remaining ponies.

Bowers later recalled:

"I heard later that Scott was very angry with me for not abandoning everything and getting away safely myself. For my own part, I must say that the abandoning of the ponies was the one thing that had never entered my head."

It was what defined men of their ilk when most ordinary men would, understandably, have been more selfish and made for a quick exit.

The floe they were on was heading in the direction of the open Ross Sea and they had to somehow discover a way back to the relative safety of solid ice. The method they adopted was to wait until an adjacent floe was close enough to drag the four sledges over. The ponies were then encouraged to jump the distance. When everything and everybody was safely landed, the process continued using the next floe. It was not without risk, and certain floes would bounce dangerously as they landed.

Having to detour westward in their attempt to reach safety was a long and arduous affair yet the location of other floes made it their only option.

One can imagine the chaos, urgency and panic of such a situation; yet, throughout an event that would reduce most to utter despair, Tom Crean remained calm and confident, as if this was just a slight hiccup unworthy of any commotion.

Bowers made a point of relaying this in his written account: *"Very little was said. Crean, like most bluejackets, behaved as if he had done this sort of thing often before."*

Bowers' short reference to Crean's unfazed demeanour provided yet another indication of the Irishman's strength of character.

Navigating between the floes, their hopes were raised when they spotted 'fast ice' (ice attached to land). Yet, no sooner had this been spotted when a further danger now entered the fray in the form of a group of killer whales. The presence of a group of orcas hunting as a pod for seals or penguins meant that the floes could be upturned at any moment. Bowers recalled a previous encounter when they were unloading the ship and when killer whales almost brought an end to the photographer Herbert Ponting's time on the expedition. Ponting escaped by the skin of his teeth as they pressed the ice beneath him forcing it to split.

The killers were a threatening sight, with their large fins circling the floes, as they let out a tremendous roar while blowing spouts of freezing seawater high into the air.

After six hours, the men reached what they assumed was a safe haven and they made their way up a large sloping floe that appeared to form part of the Barrier, the appropriately named ice shelf that prevents any vessels sailing further into the continent. Safety for the group of men, ponies and supplies, it appeared, had finally been reached.

The sense of relief, however, was short-lived, and, as they reached the top, they were met with a familiar scene. A twelve-metre wide canal of seawater lay before them, filled with fragments of brash ice-floes, all no greater than two metres in diameter, that bobbed up and down in the swell. Beyond this lay the Barrier, which formed a cliff-face fifteen to twenty feet high. To add to the hopelessness of their situation, killer whales were here, too, patrolling in search of prey.

The litany of bad fortune continued: the sloping floe they had struggled to reach split. Another dash to the safety of an adjacent floe was required. An ice sheet over 10-feet thick became their next port of call, as they gathered their equipment and dragged the sledges onto their floating camp. The three ponies were also safely manoeuvred onto the floe and the men rested for a while, deliberating their options. Two men had to remain on the floe – they would need to move again, should it break up. Only one man could leave the party of three to seek out the help they by now desperately required in order to survive.

At this juncture, Tom Crean was given the task of bringing about their rescue and, if ever a man was made for the task, he was. As Bowers watched through his telescope (not an easy task on a floating block of sea ice), Crean, using a single ski stick to steady himself, jumped from floe to floe for hours before reaching the Barrier edge. Killer whales surrounded him and one false move would have seen him become a victim to the sea beneath. He reached the edge of the barrier and scaled it before disappearing from view.

Meanwhile, Bowers and Cherry-Gerrard remained at the mercy of the elements and, at any time, they could have been blown out to sea. The survival of the remaining three ponies was of the highest priority, given the importance placed by Scott on their future role on the expedition.

The killer whales still posed a threat as they circled the floe, eyeing its residents as their next potential meal.

Bowers recalled in his account:

"We gave the ponies all they could eat that day. The Killers were too interested in us to be pleasant. They had a habit of bobbing up and down perpendicularly, so as to see over the edge of a floe, in looking for seals. Their huge black and yellow heads with sickening pig eyes only a few yards from us at times and always around us are the most disconcerting recollections I have of that day."

After reaching the top of the Barrier, Crean headed to *Safety Camp* where he and his two stranded companions had set out from the day previous. From here, Scott, Oates and Crean returned to the two stranded men who were hauled to safety along with the four sledges carrying the supplies. Scott was understandably angered by the actions of a party of men who had placed the importance of saving provisions and ponies ahead of their own survival. He was, however, relieved and Bowers remembered the moment Scott came upon the two stranded men:

"Scott, instead of blowing me up, was too relieved at our safety to be anything but pleased. I said, "What about the ponies and the sledges?" He said, "I don't give a damn about the ponies and the sledges. It's you I want and I am going to see you safe up here on the Barrier before I do anything else."

Gallant acts of selflessness were character traits shared by many during the pioneering age of discovery and being prepared to sacrifice oneself for the benefit of others was not unusual.

Crean later gave Cherry-Garrard his account of events after he set out but it was a matter-of-fact description that, in the main, detailed how he had used the ski stick to form a foothold before springing from one floe to another.

Bowers recalled:

"Crean had go up onto the Barrier at great risk to himself, as I gathered from his very modest account."

What was missing from Crean's account is better described objectively. He had shown selfless courage, regardless of the huge risks to his own life, at a time when the dangers that surrounded him were numerous.

A sad footnote to the story is that a further two of the four ponies were lost to the sea despite desperate attempts to rescue them. To lessen the suffering of two of the animals, they were killed before they descended into the waters below. It was a task those who administered the final blows found distressing but necessary. Bowers' account conveys the sad predicament of himself and Titus Oates as he tried in vain to save his charge, the pony named Uncle Bill:

"Titus said, 'He's done, we shall never get him up alive.' The cold water and shock on top of his recent troubles had been too much for the undefeated old sportsman. In vain, I tried to get him to his feet; three times he tried and, then, fell backward into the water again. At that moment, a new danger arose. The whole piece of Barrier itself started to subside.

It had evidently broken before and the tide was doing the rest. We were ordered up and it certainly was all too necessary; still, Titus and I hung over old Uncle Bill's head. I said, 'I can't leave him to be eaten alive by those whales.' There was a pick lying on the floe. Titus said, 'I shall be sick if I have to kill another horse like the last.' I had no intention that anybody should kill my own horse but myself and, getting the pick, I struck where Titus told me. I made sure of my job before we ran up and jumped the opening to the Barrier, carrying a blood-stained pickaxe instead of leading the pony I had almost considered safe."

The incident marked the first of Tom Crean's epic feats of heroism and resulted in saving the lives of two of his colleagues, whose own bravery was also to be greatly admired.

In the days when physical appearances provided reason enough to label a man with a nickname, 'Birdie' Bowers, as he was known to expedition colleagues (due to his beak-shaped nose), was to later become a member of the tragic party that Scott chose to accompany him to the South Pole. Bowers was remembered in a letter Scott wrote to Bowers' mother during the final days of his life while laying in the tent together with Bowers and Edward Wilson.

In it, he wrote:

"I write when we are very near the end of our journey and I am finishing it in company with two gallant, noble gentlemen. One of these is your son. He had come to be one of my closest and soundest friends and I appreciate his wonderful upright nature, his ability and energy. As the troubles have thickened, his dauntless spirit ever shone brighter and he has remained cheerful, hopeful and indomitable to the end."

After returning from the *Terra Nova* Expedition, Cherry-Garrard was encouraged by his friend, George Bernard Shaw, to write his own account of his time in Antarctica and the race for the Pole. *The Worst Journey in the World*, written in 1922, remains one of the most popular accounts of the expedition. His book was listed by *National Geographic* as the number one of the top 100 adventure books of all time.

Suffering psychologically for much of his life from the effects of what we now know to be Post Traumatic Stress Disorder, Apsley Cherry-Garrard passed away in 1959.

Edward Evans, recalling the story of selflessness and rescue in an address he made to the Manchester Geographical Society in 1913, said:

"They never thought of abandoning their charge, realising that Scott's polar plans might be ruined if four more ponies were lost with their sledges and equipment. Crean, with great gallantry, went for support, clambering with difficulty over the ice. He jumped from floe to floe and, at last, climbed up the face of the Barrier from a piece of ice which touched the ice cliff at the right moment... During this trying time, killer whales were about, almost continuously blowing and snorting in the intervening water spaces. Only those who have served in the Antarctic can realise fully what the party went through."[2]

Crean's actions on this occasion alone would be sufficient enough to define him a great hero but, astonishingly, he would go on to surpass this with unrivalled feats of heroism on two further rescues that brought even greater risks to himself.

*The rescue story detailed in this chapter is an adaptation of the actual events referenced from the publication in note 3 References.

Tom Crean in an image featured in the Irish Examiner, 1912
entitled: *The Kerryman With Scott*

CAPTAIN SCOTT'S PLANS.

Captain Scott, who in his memorable expedition in the Discovery, from 1901 to 1904, succeeded in going farther south than any previous explorer, left New Zealand at the end of November, 1910. He established two bases in the Antarctic, one on McMurdo Sound and the other in King Edward VII. Land, from the first of which he intended to make his dash for the Pole. His ship, the Terra Nova, returned to New Zealand last March for stores, and Captain Scott and his parties spent the summer of last year (the Antarctic winter) at their bases.

Captain Scott described his plans for the final journey in an interview before he sailed.

"The main journey," he said, "will commence in October, 1911, and it is hoped that the Pole will be reached within three months. December 22 has been suggested as a likely date upon which we may arrive at our objective. Of course, our intended journey to the Pole is dependent to a great extent on fortune. Bad weather, or an accident, would prevent full success being achieved in the present season. In that event the expedition is equipped for continuing the work in the following season.

"The main travelling party for the Pole will consist of sixteen men. After a certain distance has been traversed, four will go back, and the remainder will continue the journey. Subsequently another four will return to our base, and after one more stage has been covered a third quartet will turn round and retrace their steps northward, leaving four men to continue the last stage of the journey. No decision as to who will make up the last party of four will be arrived at until the last moment, that depending upon the physical condition of the men at the time. Obviously the fittest persons will be selected."

"SOME ANTARCTIC ARCHIVES."

Dr Edward Wilson's sketch taken from the South Polar Times.
Describing the scene he states:

*"The image represents Birdie, Crean and Cherry adrift on the floe.
It's labelled with the sign * (for ice) to prevent any mistake.
The killer whales are going for Birdie's fat legs."*

CAPTAIN SCOTT'S ANTARCTIC EXPEDITION.

Dundee, Monday.

Sir Clement Markham, who read a paper at the British Association, Dundee, on Antarctic discovery, referring to Captain Scott's journey to the South Pole said he would have arrived there about the 14th of last January. Sir Clement had reason to believe Scott's intention was to proceed along the coast as far as possible to the south, thus solving the problem of great ice barriers and ascertaining the direction of the Victorian and Edwardian mountains, and whether they united or not. One of the most valuable of Scott's results would be the complete series of meteorological, magnetic and tidal observations for four years. Scott's expedition formed the most important and fruitful enterprise ever undertaken, but there was still much to be done. Meanwhile, however, we must look forward to the next spring when the whole country would welcome the return of Captain Scott and hear of his geographical achievements with well-founded national pride.

Irish Examiner
10th September
1912

> *Whoever saves a single life,*
> *saves the world entire*

The Talmud

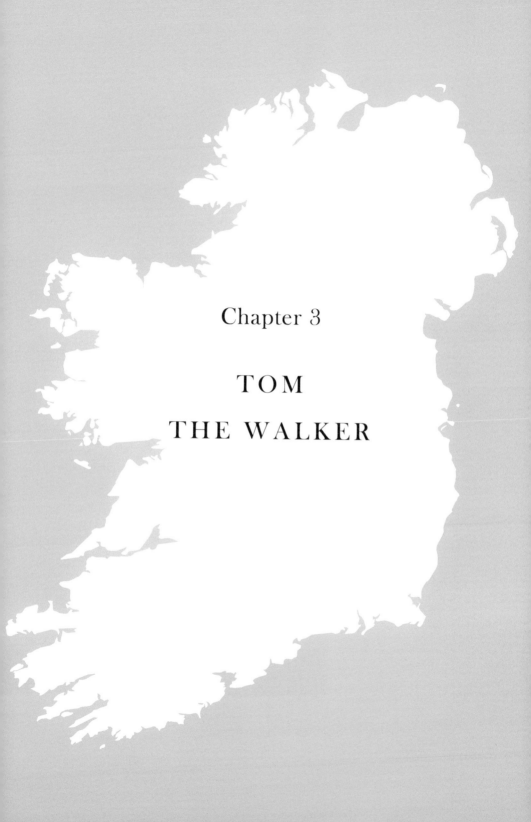

Chapter 3

TOM
THE WALKER

Between missions on the ice and to save them from boredom, expedition members would amuse themselves with various activities that reminded them of home. Donning fancy dress costumes to act out comedy dramas, going for a stroll or playing cards were among the more relaxing pastimes that brought some sense of normality to the abnormality of their surroundings.

Physical activities too kept the men in peak condition and well-prepared for the long distances that sledging missions would demand of them. Among these, soccer was a popular means of keeping the men fit and entertained during downtimes. One only has to imagine the comical nature of such an event with players slipping and sliding in pursuit of the ball.

Today the term team-building would be applied to these activities that created lasting bonds between the participants and helped to keep their spirits high in the lowest of temperatures.

Tryggve Gran, in a number of references to football-on-ice in his book, *The Norwegian with Scott*, remarked: *"Atkinson is by far the best player but Hooper, PO Evans and Crean are also quite good."*

Describing the international make-up of the teams and the daunting task an opposing team might face, Gran said:

"There was little five foot Anton our Russian groom who knew no English and had probably never even seen a football. Somewhat of a contrast were Crean and PO Evans, about six feet tall and two of the biggest men in the Navy."

Crean's sporting skills were not limited to his footballing talent and on one documented occasion he defeated Patrick Keohane to win a billiards competition. For his victory Crean won a bottle of beer but poor Keohane's forfeit was having to wear the 'Jonah medal' to signify his defeat. The significance of the term 'Jonah,' a long-established expression among sailors, translated to that of a crew member who brought bad luck and endangered a ship. To the great amusement of his colleagues and adding to the loser's ridicule, was an undertaking to announce in a loud voice, *"I am Jonah,"* before sitting down to eat lunch with the other members of the expedition. The entertaining spectacle would continue until the medal was inherited by the next defeated recipient.

Giving the title to the runner-up of a billiard tournament was stretching the term somewhat but extreme bad luck was what the *Terra Nova* expedition would most be remembered for.

The journey to the Pole had commenced on 24th October 1911. With sixteen men in teams of four, the first team - comprising of Teddy Evans, William Lashly, Frederick Hooper and Bernard Day - started the trek on the two motor sledges but, fifty miles into their journey, the machines failed and the team abandoned the unreliable machines in favour of man-hauling.

Scott and the remaining three teams set out on 1st November.

After the second support team of Apsley Cherry-Garrard, Charles Wright, Edward Atkinson and Patsy Keohane had been returned on 22nd December, the remaining eight were very nearly reduced to seven on Christmas Day after having reached the polar plateau.

Lashly, who was celebrating his birthday, fell into a huge crevasse and, in the process, his sharp fall jerked Bowers and Crean, both harnessed to the same sledge, backwards. Lashly was left precariously dangling at the end of a strained Alpine rope part way down a fifty-foot-deep chasm.

As the safety of their colleague was literally hanging in the balance, Lashly's drop had jammed Crean's harness under the sledge which was hanging over the crevasse. Teddy Evans and Bowers managed to free it and all three men were now in a race to save their hanging companion. Lashly, hidden from view by an overhanging mound of ice, shouted up to alert his colleagues that he was still in the land of the living and the three rescuers hauled their relieved colleague to safety. Lashly's 44th birthday had been a memorable one and could have been the last one he ever celebrated.

On 4th January 1912, Captain Scott and the party of seven men reached a point of 168 statute miles from the South Pole. The prize of being the first men to reach the South Pole was within sight and Scott made his final choice about who would accompany him on the journey. He was fully expected to take three men, making up a party of four, but he defied convention at this late stage. Five men would make the final assault and, as he deliberated who to choose, the group waited to learn of their fate.

Since their first foray to the South Pole in 1901, Tom Crean, having served under Scott on all of his naval postings prior to this, his second expedition, was widely expected to accompany his Captain on the path to glory.

Scott's second in command, Lieutenant Teddy Evans, had expected to be included but Scott considered that his exhaustion, following the draining journey up to this point, would render him and Lashly in no fit state to journey to the Pole and back. It was perhaps understandable given that both men had man-hauled substantially more than the rest of the party after the motors had seized up.

In breaking the disappointing news to Crean and by way of explanation for his exclusion, Scott made use of a harmless cough Tom had. Bitterly disappointed, Crean was in little doubt that Scott had found the poorest of excuses and said: *"I understand a half-song when I hear one, sir."*

The downcast trio accompanied Scott's group for three miles before bidding them farewell. Crean wept as the final team of Scott, Henry Bowers, Lawrence Oates, Edward Wilson and his great friend, Edgar Evans, disappeared into the mist on what was to be both a disappointing and fateful last mission for all five men.

Crean, Lashly and Teddy Evans faced a daunting and dangerous 800-mile trek back to the safety of *Hut Point*. To put this into perspective, the trip they were facing would be the equivalent of walking from Dublin to Killarney four times over at the mercy of fierce blizzards and in conditions far colder than in a typical freezer.

With thick snow underfoot, mountainous ice paths and pressure ridges to negotiate, hidden crevasses to avoid, and with a heavy sledge and provisions in tow, just imagining such a journey would surely strike fear into the toughest of people.

Scott's decision to take four men with him to the Pole made the journey of the return party even more difficult, as, up to this point, four-man teams had grown used to hauling the sledges.

The progress of the three-man team would be slower and Evans had calculated that a march of seventeen miles per day would allow them to remain on schedule without running short on food supplies before reaching the provision depots that were strategically located on their return. After making a late start on their first day, the party made a distance of approximately thirteen miles and for the entire journey back, distances would remain approximate as they had no sledge metre.

The following day, they trekked the necessary mileage but the surface was not very good and their daily distances thereafter were reducing because of worsening weather and poor visibility. Crean, who had been leading the group, suffered an attack of snow blindness and Lashly had to replace him in the leading position on 6*th* January, at which point they had reached *3-Degree Depot* on schedule.

By 10*th* January, provisions were running low and they had to make better progress in order to reach the next depot. Crean's eyes had, by this stage, recovered but making the required distances had proven difficult and supplies were running low.

The thin air of the polar plateau further hampered their progress and all three men suffered from shortness of breath. To make matters worse, poor visibility and blizzards now led them off course and they found themselves at the top of the Shackleton Ice Falls.

In an attempt to compensate for lost time, on 11*th* January, they decided to sledge down from the polar plateau in order to recover their route onto the *Beardmore Glacier*. It was a huge risk and they would have to negotiate pressure ridges and ice mounds. The sledge reached speeds of almost 60mph as they sped down but, with great fortune, all three survived the ride unscathed, aside from a few bruises. Their gamble had saved them three days' journey time and the equivalent in food supplies.

Evans later recalled:

"On the return journey, the soft snow was further hampering our progress and the outlook was so bad we cut corners."

He continued;

"This led us over Shackleton Ice Falls at the head of the Beard-more Glacier. We descended many hundreds of feet mostly riding on the sledge; we had frequent capsizes and broke the bow of the sledge. Crean had the misfortune to catch his trousers somehow in our headlong flight and they were torn to shreds."[1]

They now faced a descent down the 125-mile glacier route that would lead them to the Great Ice Barrier. As they continued their journey, crevasses were now becoming more of a frequent danger and there was no let-up in the bad weather conditions but, despite the obstacles they were facing, they were achieving an average of 15 miles per day.

On 14th January, they reached *Mount Darwin Depot (aka Upper Glacier depot)*, where they stocked up on their food supplies and took a much-needed break. Crean took the time to replace his shredded trousers with a pair of Mandleberg wind-proofs he had previously left in the depot cairn. After eating lunch, they continued their march down the glacier.

They, again, encountered a number of ice crevasses but they made better headway having picked up crampons at the depot.

After a rough night in camp on 16th January, the following day brought more misery as they struggled through another blizzard to be confronted with a further obstacle to their progress. It came in the form of a huge ice chasm with only a narrow ice bridge spanning its width. By now, it seemed as if the odds were stacked against them and that their hopeless fate was sealed.

After some contemplation of the task ahead, Lashly, with an Alpine rope tied around his waist, shuffled across, his legs astride the bridge. He dared not look down to the depths below and, laboriously, he made it to the other side. There now remained the small matter of hauling a

400lb sledge which was in the hands of Crean and Evans. Only one of the sledge's runners was able to fit on the narrow ice track; so, facing one another on either side, the two men gingerly heaved it across the bridge lopsided, little by little.

Silence ensued as they considered their fate should they lose their balance until, finally, Lashly's hand was within reach. Both men wriggled their way off the bridge and onto safe ground with their foot crampons gripping into solid ground. All could have been lost as, simultaneously, the sledge plunged into the crevasse. Still attached to the rope the three used their dwindling reserves of strength to haul it back up.

As the trio slumped exhausted on the sledge, their position appeared increasingly hopeless as they surveyed the littered route of crevasses and pressure ridges ahead of them. By now, they were in urgent need of nourishment following their ordeal; yet, there was no suitable place to pitch the tent and food provisions were low.

Evans went ahead to assess the best path and, at one point, turned around to see the figures of Crean and Lashly hauling the sledge in the distance.

In his book *South with Scott*, he recalled:

"I felt a tremendous love for those two men that day. They had trusted me implicitly and believed in my ability to win through."

Valleys of ice now lay in their path and Evans continued ahead seeking out the best route. Suddenly, upon reaching the top of an ice slope, he spotted *Cloudmaker Depot* in the distance. A smooth plain of ice stretched out before him.

Elated, he returned to his companions and broke the good news. They decided it was the right time to set up camp and soon finished off the last of their food and drink provisions.

Their luck, it appeared, had changed.

Morale was high and Evans drooled over the thought of enjoying one of Lashly's legendary steak and kidney puddings on their return to base.

After a particularly bad day on 18th January, they reached *Cloudmaker Depot (aka Mid Glacier Depot)*, exhausted after another energy-sapping haul.

Having removed his goggles to survey the course ahead of them the previous day, Evans consequently suffered from a painful bout of snow blindness that would stay with him for almost a fortnight. Lashly, in his diary, made his first reference to what would signal the start of Evan's descent into ill-health at a time when there was still a further 400 miles to cover:

"Evans had his goggles off all day to pick out the course over the crevasses and he suffered agony of snow blindness for the next fortnight. He was unable to write his diary up again until 29th January. He was too blind to do any useful pulling and could only walk along beside the sledge."

Continuing their journey with Evans still unable to see, they made *Lower Glacier Depot* on 21st January.

There was small cause for celebration on the 22nd as their days on the *Beardmore Glacier* were coming to an end. When they caught sight of the *Great Ice Barrier* below, Crean let out a huge celebratory yell that Lashly remarked was *"enough to frighten the ponies out of their graves."* After descending the *Beardmore* onto the Barrier, they reached *South Barrier Depot*, where they replenished food supplies and changed the sledge.

On 23rd January, Evans had now recovered his sight and appeared to be over his sufferings.

The weather presented them with higher temperatures over the following days and, after reaching *Mid Barrier Depot* and taking to their skis, they made good progress averaging around 14 miles a day.

27th January was a particularly warm day and Lashly remarked that they could have removed their clothes and marched on. With a good breeze behind them, pulling the sledge took little effort and was made easier with the sail up.

The sentiment of better fortune did not last long though, and it was on the same day that Evans displayed the further signs of physical suffering with severe loosening of the bowels.

It had been a week since Evans had recovered from the effects of snow blindness; yet, on 30th January, he complained of stiffness in his legs and there was no improvement in his bowel condition. Crean had suffered similarly days earlier but he was over it by this stage. It was decided to stop feeding Evans the Pemmican and, in an effort to improve his condition, he was given a drop of brandy, some chalk and opium pills.

Throughout their journey back, the group had left notes at each of the depots to update Scott and his party who would be taking the same route back. Unaware of whether their colleagues had won the race to reach the Pole, the three men took great care to ensure that provisions were sufficient and in good order for the return trip of Scott.

By 4th February, they reached *Mount Hooper Depot* and were within 180 miles of their destination. The condition of Evans, however, had worsened and it was clear he was showing all the signs of scurvy.

By now, he was virtually invalided. Still suffering from looseness of the bowels, he was barely shuffling along with the aid of a ski stick. The disease was advancing rapidly. His teeth loosened and his gums had become sore and ulcerated.

On 9th February, they reached *One Ton Depot*, where a change of food was most welcome from the monotonous diet they had to endure to this point. 120 miles now separated them from *Hut Point* and reaching it as soon as possible had become a matter of urgency. Evans was still barely on his legs but his condition was declining and progress was painfully slow. To make matters worse, the temperature was dropping.

With a marked deterioration in Evans' condition, they ground to a halt on 13th February. His pain was severe, his legs were green and swollen, and he was so weak he ordered his two companions to abandon him and save themselves. He had not accounted, though, for the resoluteness and honour of the men that stood before him and, steadfastly, they refused.

It was, he later recounted: *"the first and last time my orders as a naval Officer had been disobeyed."* The two men placed their sick colleague on the sledge, attached their harnesses and trudged on.

Two exhausted men were now pulling a sledge designed to be hauled by four with the additional weight of a sick patient. It made their task seem impossible but Lashly and Crean, despite their severely reduced strength, were sledge-hauling veterans. Evans was fortunate that his two companions were considered among the most powerful men in the expedition's crew.

The pair marched on with their patient in tow but were forced to stop once again on 17th February. They were almost spent; yet, having hauled Evans on the sledge for 38 miles, their mental resolve remained high as Lashly remarked:

"We are pretty tired tonight. I don't think we have got the go in us as we had but we must try and push on."

By now, the worsening conditions of the viciously cold Antarctic blizzards put paid to any further progress. They set up camp for the night just a mile away from *Corner Camp*. They were 35 miles short of *Hut Point*, their destination and place of safety.

On the morning of 18th February, after a night through which his protective companions kept a careful watch on him, Evans fainted. Crean and Lashly rushed to his aid and Crean, thinking his commander had died, cradled him in his arms.

Evans later recalled: *"His hot tears fell on my face and, as I came to, I gave a weak kind of laugh."*

It was futile to think they could continue as they comforted their critically ill patient. It appeared Evans' quest for life was now nearing an end. The only option left was for one of the men to set out for *Hut Point* while the other remained in the tent and tended to Evans. On what appeared a fine day, Crean volunteered and, with two biscuits and a stick of chocolate to fuel his march for life, he set forth on a mission that would see his journey enter the annals of history.

William Lashly's role now was to nurse Evans and keep him alive in the hope that Crean would make it but the omens did not look good for that outcome.

Shortly after Crean departed, Lashly made a dash for *Corner Camp* to gather any provisions that may help his quest to keep Evans alive. He returned with food and a large piece of bamboo on which he tied a flag before fastening it to the sledge. Most worryingly though, he had discovered a note left there by Bernard Day, the expedition's motor engineer, warning that the route between their location and sea was littered with dangerous crevasses - this was the direction Tom Crean would have travelled.

Crean had set out on foot and that made him far more vulnerable than if he had travelled on ski.

Wisely, Lashly omitted to pass that information on to Evans who needed news of a better kind.

A reliable, first-hand account of Tom Crean's 18-hour trek was transcribed in an account given to Apsley Cherry-Garrard for his classic book, *The Worst Journey in the World*:

> *"He'd started out at 10 a.m. on Sunday morning and 'the surface was good, very good surface indeed', and he went about 16 miles before he stopped. He had three biscuits and two sticks of chocolate. He stopped about five minutes, sitting on the snow, and ate two biscuits and the chocolate, and put one biscuit back in his pocket. He was quite warm and not sleepy.*
>
> *He carried on just the same and passed Safety Camp on his right some five hours later, and thinks it was about 12:30 that he reached the edge of the Barrier, tired, getting cold in the back and the weather coming on thick. It was bright behind him and it was coming over the Bluff and White Island was obscured, though he could still see Cape Armitage and Castle Rock. He slipped a lot on the sea-ice, having several falls on to his back and it was getting thicker all the time. At the Barrier edge, there was a light wind, now it was blowing a strong wind, drifting and snowing. He made for the Gap and could not get up at first. To avoid taking a lot out of himself, he started to go round Cape Armitage but soon felt slush coming through his finnesko boots (he had no crampons) and made back for the Gap. He climbed*

*up to the left of the Gap and climbed along the side of Obser-
vation Hill to avoid the slippery ice. When he got to the top, it
was clear enough to see vaguely the outline of Hut Point but
he could see no sledges nor dogs. He sat down under the lee of
Observation Hill and finished his last biscuit with a bit of ice.
'I was very dry' - he slid down the side of Observation Hill and
thought at this time there was open water below, for he had no
goggles on the march and his eyes were strained. But, on getting
near the ice-foot, he found it was polished sea-ice and made his
way round to the hut under the ice-foot. When he got close, he
saw the dogs and sledges on the sea-ice and it was now blowing
very hard with drift."*

On 19th February 1912 at 3:30 a.m., an exhausted, shivering,
lone figure entered the expedition base at *Hut Point*. Tom Crean had
just completed his incredible 35-mile journey on meagre rations. He
had marched for eighteen hours under the most hazardous and extreme conditions on earth and he had undertaken the journey with
one thought in his mind - to save a life, regardless that he risked his
own to do so.

His colleagues at the hut - Edward Atkinson, the expedition's
doctor, and the Russian dog leader, Dimitri Gerov - sat him down,
gave him a nip of brandy and a bowl of porridge but he could not keep
it down. The rigours of his remarkable trek had left him physically
drained. Outside, a storm was raging that prevented the immediate
rescue of the two stranded men. The blizzards remained until the following day when it abated. It was the window they had waited for and
Atkinson and Dimitri immediately loaded their sledges in readiness
to perform the rescue.

Amazingly, Tom Crean, fresh from his energy-sapping mission

undertaken after being out on the ice for three-and-a-half months, had asked to join them in the rescue. Atkinson flatly refused and, at 4:30 pm on 20th February, he and Dimitri set off.

Upon reaching the tent, they fed Lashly and provided Evans a specially prepared hot meal, before laying both men on the sledges and making for home.

The doctor, Atkinson, later told Cherry-Garrard that, when he first saw the condition of Evans, he felt he was certain to die and, had the rescue been delayed another day, there is little doubt he would have.

Crean's heroism did not go unnoticed by his colleagues. Years later, in 1939, writing in appreciation of Crean after he had died, Frank Debenham, an Australian geologist who served alongside him on the *Terra Nova* expedition and who later became the first director of The Scott Polar Research Institute, stated:

"His amazing walk of 35 miles to get help at the end, on the top of a journey of some four months, is one of the unforgettable classics among polar feats."[2]

Crean's extraordinary powers of endurance had proved pivotal in saving the life of Scott's second in command, Lieutenant Edward Evans. Equal credit in the saving of Evans' life has to go to William Lashly, who kept his patient alive until their safe rescue.

Both Crean and Lashly were later awarded the Albert Medal for bravery for their heroic life-saving feat. Lieutenant Edward Evans, who went on to become a Vice-Admiral, never forgot Crean and Lashly, the two men he owed his life to. Expressing his gratitude to them, he said *"they had the Hearts of Lions."*

Tom Crean had one final mission before his return home aboard *Terra Nova*. He was a member of the search party that found the bodies of Scott, Wilson and Bowers on 12th November 1912. They lay beside one another in the tent that saw them draw their last breaths. They had reached the South Pole but worsening conditions on their return confined them in the shelter of their tent where a shortage of food and supplies decided their fate. Agonisingly, they were just 11 miles short of *One Ton Depot* and safety. Crean had lost a good friend in Scott and stated *"I loved every hair on his head."*

Immediately as he stepped outside of the tent Crean strode up to Gran and the Norwegian recalled:

*"Tom Crean came over to me and said, Sir, permit me to congrat-ulate you. Dr Atkinson has just found Scott's diary where it is writ-ten that our people found the Norwegian flag when they came to the South Pole. I grasped the outstretched hand, shook it and gazed into his tearful eyes. Then I too was overcome with emotion."*3

The search party removed three notebooks from a wallet rest-ing under Scott's shoulder. They contained a number of letters and Scott's diary. An emotional burial service was read out before cov-ering the bodies with the tent and building a large snow cairn above it. Upon this, Gran - the sole Norwegian member of the expedition whose countryman, Amundsen, had beaten Scott to the pole - placed his skis in the form of a cross.

Terra Nova, with her sail at half-mast, sailed quietly into the New Zealand port of Oamaru at 2:30 a.m. on 10th February, where the crew were under orders not to answer any questions from wait-ing reporters. From here, a boat was lowered and Atkinson and Lieu-tenant Pennell were rowed ashore. From there, they boarded a train to Christchurch and cabled the news to London. Crean, one of the boat's crew, later announced that they had been shadowed by a group of journalists eager to know more. All questions were met with silence and the first news editions reported that it was Scott and a fellow officer who had left the ship.[4]

Readers discovered the truth the following day when the world first learned of the tragedy.

On 12th February 1913, the ship made her way into Lyttelton to undergo a refit before the journey back to Britain. A hurriedly arranged memorial service to Scott and his dead comrades was held at St Paul's Cathedral two days later, where thousands lined the streets to pay their respects to the brave, tragic explorers.[5] The same day, it was reported that a joint proposal for Australia and New Zealand to charter the *Terra Nova* to recover the bodies of Scott and his party for burial in St Paul's Cathedral was rejected by members of the expedition. They stated that, had it been thought right to bring the bodies back, Commander Evans would have done so. Had the retrieval mission gone ahead, *Terra Nova* would have been under the command of Sir Ernest Shackleton.[6]

There followed an inquest by the media questioning why the party were not rescued and that debate still rages to this day, where controversial accusations resurface blaming one member of the expedition or another for the demise of the leader and his team. The facts, though, speak far louder than the assumptions and they can be found within Scott's last message to the public:

"I maintain that our arrangements for returning were quite adequate and that no one in the world would have expected the temperatures and surfaces which we encountered at this time of the year. On the summit in lat. 85° 86° we had -20°, -30°. On the Barrier in lat. 82°, 10,000 feet lower, we had -30° in the day, -47° at night pretty regularly, with continuous headwind

during our day marches. It is clear that these circumstances come on very suddenly and our wreck is certainly due to this sudden advent of severe weather, which does not seem to have any satisfactory cause. I do not think human beings ever came through such a month as we have come through, and we should have got through in spite of the weather but for the sickening of a second companion, Captain Oates, and a shortage of fuel in our depots for which I cannot account and, finally, but for the storm which has fallen on us within 11 miles of the depot at which we hoped to secure our final supplies. Surely, misfortune could scarcely have exceeded this last blow.

We arrived within 11 miles of our old One Ton Camp with fuel for one last meal and food for two days. For four days, we have been unable to leave the tent – the gale howling about us."

The reference to a shortage of fuel in Scott's letter had been caused by evaporation due to inefficient sealing of the fuel cans. Unaccountable fuel loss was a phenomenon that had been experienced on previous expeditions and Amundsen had learned from this, ensuring his cans were hermetically sealed with specially designed bungs. In contrast, Scott's expedition used a leather washer to seal the cans. It was the deterioration of these washers that allowed the fuel to evaporate. The same was discovered by Crean, Lashly and Evans on their return journey; yet, for Scott's party, the raging blizzard outside their tent prevented any further progress. Without fuel for food and warmth and with temperatures regularly plummeting below -30°, their fate was sealed.

It was the nature of Antarctica, not the nature of man that was to blame.

On 21ˢᵗ May 1913, Commander Evans took to the stage to a rapturous welcome at a packed Royal Albert Hall in London. On the platform with him were 11 members of the expedition including Cherry-Garrard, Cecil Meares, Edward Atkinson, Herbert Ponting and Tryggve Gran. Lady Scott, Mrs Wilson and Mrs Evans, the widows of three of the polar party, were also in attendance, along with Captain Oates' mother.[7]

Evans gave a two-hour account of the trials and tribulations of the expedition assisted by slides fed to a giant screen.

Although Lashly and Crean were not present, they were very much there in spirit, as Evans displayed both men's images separately after summarising the return journey of the last support party to a hushed audience. In eulogising the two men who saved his life, he said:

"This is Lashly. He is a Chief Stoker in the Royal Navy and has been a teetotaller and non-smoker all his life."

With Crean's image now projected to the screen, he continued:

"This is a very good picture of Crean. He was Captain Scott's coxswain in his last two ships - a great, big, enthusiastic Irishman who, many times, distinguished himself in this expedition. Both of these men have been recommended for the Albert Medal."

With his lecture proving a great success, Evans later went on a tour which, at the end of October 1913, saw him take to the stage at Manchester's *Free Trade Hall*[8] to address the Manchester Royal Geographic Society. He, again, praised the immense courage of the two men who showed almost *"superhuman endurance"* to save his life. Again, displaying the images of both men in the background to another packed audience, he paid his tributes. As Lashly's image came up on screen, he began with a familiar commentary:

"It may interest you to know that Lashly has been a teetotaller and a non-smoker all his life."

The crowds applauded loudly before Evans continued, as the image of Crean popped up:

"It may interest others to know that Crean had been neither."

At this, the audience burst out into great laughter.

The gratitude of Evans was lifelong and, when he wrote his own account, *South with Scott,* in 1922, the words: *"To Lashly and Crean, this book is affectionately dedicated,"* were written in remembrance of the two men who saved his life.

On 14th June 1913, *Terra Nova* arrived home to Cardiff.

Teddy, now Commander Evans, had earlier rejoined having taken charge of the ship at the Isles of Scilly. Shortly after noon the ship headed into Bute Dock from where she'd left 3 years earlier and thousands had turned out to welcome the ship home.

Earlier that morning, a tug boat had sailed out from Pentarth Pier to meet Terra

St Paul's Burial Proposal

'Members of the expedition do not favour the suggestion that Australia and New Zealand should charter the *Terra Nova*, put Sir Ernest Shackleton in command, and send her to procure the bodies of Captain Scott and his party for burial in St Paul's Cathedral.

They say, if it had been thought right to bring the bodies back, Commander Evans would have done so.'

Ballarat Star,
February 15th, 1913

Nova. Among its passengers were two of the widows, Lady Scott and Mrs Oriana Wilson. Scott's young son Peter, just two months short of his 4th birthday, was carried aboard the polar vessel by one of the sailors. "*Isn't my daddy here?*" he asked.[9]

The sailor, reportedly, turned away and his eyes filled with tears. Commander Evans came briskly forward to save the situation with: "*Hello old fellow and how are you?*" it was enough to distract the youngster and he set about excited exploration of his father's ship.[10]

No-one more than Evans would have remembered the past year with so heavy a heart. With his life hanging by a thread on the torturous return journey from the Polar plateau with Crean and Lashly, he was fortunate to be standing at the helm of the ship this day. The world had learned of Amundsen's triumph on 7th March 1912 and returning with *Terra Nova* to Antarctica in January 1913, Evans had expectations of greeting the Polar party and offering his sympathies for their failure to be the first to reach the Pole. Instead his return was met with the news that they had perished.

It was enough to sink most men to the depths of despair but to add more heavily to his woes, his greatest loss would occur just three months later as he journeyed ahead of *Terra Nova's* return to Cardiff. Accompanying her husband aboard the steam passenger liner *Otranto* bound for London, was his wife Hilda.

On the 14th April she had taken seriously ill aboard the ship as it approached the Port of Naples. As her condition worsened an emergency operation was carried out aboard the ship yet she died on the 18th April. Evans had witnessed the efforts to save his wife yet she had contracted peritonitis. After the ship reached Toulon she was laid to rest.[11]

As the *Terra Nova* slowly approached her berth at Roath Basin a wave of emotion passed through the crowd who let out a subdued cheer to welcome home the forlorn crew.

The officers and crew stood silently in reaction - for them, there was little cause to celebrate having arrived back without their captain and five of their colleagues.

Adding to the fatalities of the ill-fated expedition, Stoker and Petty Officer Robert Brissenden, a member of the ship's party, had drowned a year earlier while on a survey cruise in the French Pass in New Zealand.[12]

It was a strange homecoming where a mixture of emotions played out among all who had congregated at the dock. As the men gathered together for photographs, the sadness was never more evident than on the faces of Lashly, Evans and Crean, who reluctantly posed for photographs and who were the last three men to have seen the Polar party alive.

For a brief time the mood altered as one of the 12 dogs who'd been returned on the ship, (of 35 dogs who'd left three years earlier), broke free of its restraints and bolted down the dockside, scattering the startled onlookers. However, on hearing the whistle of its master, the ship's surgeon, Edward Atkinson, the animal turned and slowly made its way back, head bowed and with its tail between its legs.[13]

The following day the men attended a solemn church service at St Stephens Church and on Monday, 16th June, the crew and officers attended the Coal Exchange for a reception given in their honour by the merchants of Cardiff whose financial contributions had made the expedition possible. In his speech, the Lord Mayor paid homage to *"the heroes who had sacrificed their lives in the Scott expedition."* It was a poignant reminder of loss to all who were gathered there, among them, sat in the gallery, was Lois Evans, widow of Edgar.

Later that evening the crew attended a banquet given in their honour at the city's Royal Hotel.[14]

The sombre homecoming had provided Tom Crean with an opportunity to offer his deepest sympathies to the loved ones of his lost friends.

Tom Crean's bravery was later rewarded in a medal presentation at Buckingham Palace on 26th July 1913 and it was recommended that his promotion to Chief Petty Officer be backdated to 9th September 1910.

In the story that overshadowed Crean's epic solo march to save Edward Evans, another Evans, Crean's great friend, the Welshman, Edgar Evans, would not survive the journey back.

Unable to keep up with the rest of the party due to a head injury he sustained after falling into a crevasse on 4th February, the Welshman's condition, both mentally and physically, deteriorated rapidly. The others returned to fetch him and found him in a dreadful condition with severely frostbitten hands, head bowed and on his knees. They placed him on a sledge and he was taken back to the tent they had erected. By the time they had reached camp, he was comatose. Nothing could be done to save him and he died on 17th February 1912.

Although he was in the company of Captain Scott and the return party at the time of his passing, the location of Evans' body was never discovered. He had earlier confided in Crean that, upon his return, he would like to open a pub on the beautiful Gower Peninsula that was his home. It could be considered that Crean's decision to open his own bar was, in part, homage to his friend and, today, Annascaul's *South Pole Inn*, whose first publican was Tom Crean, remains a busy attraction.

The fate of Captain Lawrence Oates is one that remains immortalised by his last words. On the return journey of the polar party, he suffered from severe frostbite to his feet and his worsening condition hampered the progress of the three remaining members now desperate to reach safety.

Approximately 30 miles short of *One Ton Depot* and having to set up camp due to worsening conditions, Oates left the tent. It was the morning of 17th March 1912 and, outside, a blizzard was raging in temperatures of -40°F.

In what has been considered the ultimate act of self-sacrifice for the benefit of his companions, his departing words were: *"I am just going outside and may be some time."* The brave officer of the 6th Inniskilling Dragoons, who had been left with his left leg an inch shorter than his right after suffering a gunshot wound in 1901, drew his last breath on St Patrick's Day, which also happened to be his birthdate. He was 32 years old.

Delivered very fittingly, again on St Patrick's Day two years later, to a packed audience at Carnegie Hall in New York, Edward Evans gave an enthralling account of the expedition and of its fateful outcome. A transcript of his lecture featured prominently in the New York Times the following day and, again, he took the opportunity to tell his audience of the heroes who saved his life:

> *"They are the men to whom I owe my life and braver, nobler fellows have never lived than they. Crean was Scott's coxswain on his ship and I am glad to say that he has since been decorated by King George for saving my life. When I begged them to leave me, it was Crean who, speaking for both, turned and said to me, 'If you are to go out sir, then we'll all go out together."*

Edward Evans' distinguished naval career after the expedition would see him rise to the rank of Admiral in 1936. Later, in 1945, he was made a Peer: the first Baron Mountevans of Chelsea. In a heroic act, reminiscent of that from which he himself had benefitted, Evans, then captain of *HMS Carlisle*, on 3rd March 1921, swam to the rescue of passengers of a Singapore passenger ship, *SS Hung Moh,* after it struck rocks and broke in two. He hauled many of the passengers to safety aboard motor boats attached to his ship and, for his bravery, was awarded the Silver Medal for Gallantry in saving life at sea.[15] He died on 20th August 1957.

William Lashly retired from the navy after his return but re-joined as a naval reserve and served in the First World War and later as a Customs officer, before retiring in 1932. Lashly's accounts of the two expeditions on which he served were edited and published in 1969, and *Under Scott's Command* remains a rare source of the *Discovery* and *Terra Nova* expeditions from the perspective of a naval rating. George Skinner and his wife Valerie, a descendant of Lashly, later updated his story and *The Life and Adventures of William Lashly* is a comprehensive study of his life. William died in his home village of Hambledon, near Portsmouth, on 12th June 1940.[16]

The sad fate of Scott and the four men he chose to accompany him to the pole understandably overshadowed the drama played out on the return journey, and little coverage was given to the heroic feats of Lashly and Crean. In the years to follow, there was little change, as the story of the race to the Pole and the sad demise of the five men on their return journey grew in legend. Undoubtedly, this was a primary factor that served to keep Crean's story in the shadows until the turn of the following century.

Some years ago, on a visit to Annascaul, the son of Edward Evans, Broke Evans, put it quite simply, saying, *"If it wasn't for Tom Crean, I wouldn't be here."* It was to be a sentiment felt by many more descendants, as Crean's last expedition alongside Sir Ernest Shackleton was to prove.

The rescue story detailed in this chapter is an adaptation of the actual events referenced from the publication in notes 17 and 18 References.

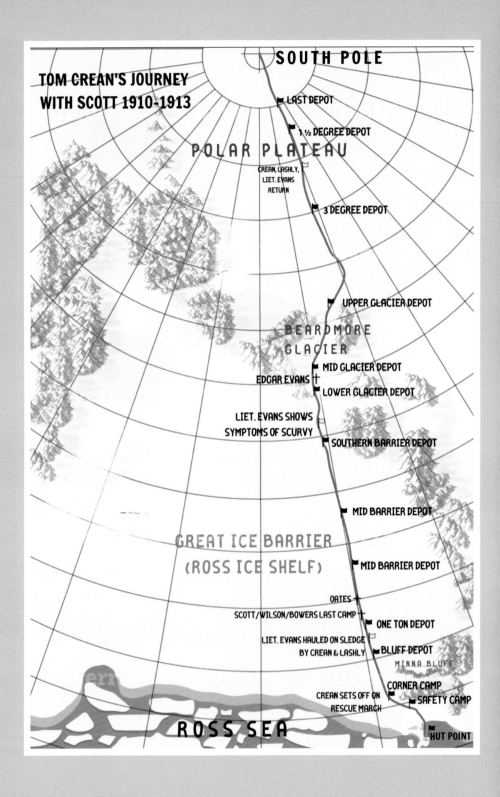

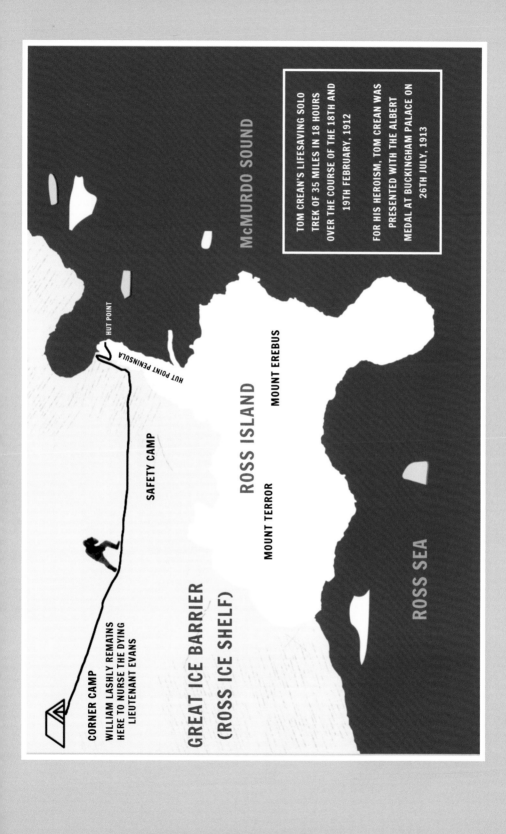

CORNER CAMP
WILLIAM LASHLY REMAINS
HERE TO NURSE THE DYING
LIEUTENANT EVANS

SAFETY CAMP

GREAT ICE BARRIER
(ROSS ICE SHELF)

HUT POINT

HUT POINT PENINSULA

McMURDO SOUND

ROSS ISLAND

MOUNT TERROR

MOUNT EREBUS

ROSS SEA

TOM CREAN'S LIFESAVING SOLO
TREK OF 35 MILES IN 18 HOURS
OVER THE COURSE OF THE 18TH AND
19TH FEBRUARY, 1912

FOR HIS HEROISM, TOM CREAN WAS
PRESENTED WITH THE ALBERT
MEDAL AT BUCKINGHAM PALACE ON
26TH JULY, 1913

THE SCOTT ANTARCTIC DISASTER.

INTERVIEW WITH COMMANDER EVANS.

(CENTRAL NEWS SPECIAL CORRESPONDENT.)

PORT SAID. SUNDAY NIGHT.

The Orient liner Otranto from Australian ports arrived here to-day, having on board Commander Evans, whose cablegrams from Christchurch first gave to the world the story of the disaster to Captain Scott's Antarctic expedition.

Commander Evans was first told of some of the rumours which were circulated regarding the fate of Seaman Edgar Evans, and was asked whether there was really any mystery concerning his death, or the circumstances which preceded it. He replied that nothing had been withheld from the press regarding Evans's fate.

The Fate of Evans.

"Poor Evans behaved magnificently throughout the expedition," he said, "and his astonishing failure, as Captain Scott describes it, was due to the continuous hardships encountered. Evans was possessed of tremendous strength, but it would seem that his staying power was not equal to that of his tent-mates. It is possible that he developed scurvy, but of that I have no knowledge. Our information concerning the loss of the Southern party is somewhat meagre. The diaries of our five lost companions are being handed to their nearest relatives, and the members of the expedition have not had access to them. Dr. Atkinson, who was in charge of the search party, read that part of Captain Scott's diary immediately concerned with the fate of the Southern party and Lady Scott has read the extracts from her husband's diary. owever, let us return to your questions with reference to Seaman Evans."

I quoted a sentence from his cablegram. "He (Seaman Evans) was a great anxiety to them on the plateau," and asked for the exact meaning of the sentence. Was there any friction between Evans and the other members of the party?—"I know there was certainly no such friction," replied Commander Evans. "The other members of the Polar party, it is true, were delayed by his serious condition, particularly after he sustained concussion, but there was no friction."

I pointed out that members of the expedition had been quoted in the press as saying that Evans, at any rate temporarily, became insane. "I do not believe it for a moment," was the reply, "and rumours to that effect should be contradicted."

"Is it a fact," I asked, "that Evans had virtually to be carried by his comrades on the plateau?"—"He was not carried on the sledge except on the day he died," was the reply.

Search Parties' Efforts.

Commander Evans was next questioned as to the efforts made to relieve the Southern party. Speaking with reference to the journey undertaken by Mr. Cherry Garrard and Demetri, who were the first to start on a relief expedition but were forced to return from the One Ton Camp (eleven miles from the scene of the final tragedy) Commander Evans said: "Garrard and Demetri experienced the same abnormally severe weather which Captain Scott speaks about. The dog marches suffered in consequence, and they could not dash blindly forward in driving snow. There were only two other men at Hut Point, for the ship had left some time before."

Again quoting Commander Evans's cablegram, I spoke of the second relief expedition, that of Atkinson and Kohane, which fought its way out to Corner Camp and there realised that it could be of no assistance. "When Atkinson and Keohane set out" said the Commander, "they were much handicapped by the bad surfaces and severe weather conditions that obtained. They pulled their sledges sixty-eight miles with the greatest difficulty. It was a forlorn hope from the start."

"Would it have made any difference to the ultimate tragedy," I asked, "if this relief party had gone on instead of coming back?"—"I can only say," he answered, "that no two men in our expedition if they had gone on further could have brought themselves back, far less help an exhausted party into camp. Had they pushed further south we should have lost seven men instead of five. In these low temperatures we used to collect so much ice in our equipment that weights increased enormously. To give you an example. In the splendid winter journey undertaken by Wilson, Bowers, and Garrard the weights of their sleeping-bags increased from .47lb. at starting to 118lb., other weights increasing in the same proportion. This unavoidable increase in weights materially shortened the marches."

Details of the Last Scenes.

I ventured to remark that little had been said in detail as to the scenes of the final stage of the search made by the party which found the bodies. "We do not wish to add any details in this connection," said the Commander.

"It has been suggested," I said, "that some of the features of the tragedy have been deliberately suppressed." "It is quite wrong to suggest such a thing," he replied. "Captain Scott's tent, in which the bodies were found, was sighted on November 12 last year. The bodies were naturally very emaciated. The men had obviously died, as reported in my first telegram, of starvation and exposure."

"Is it true that Scott and the others left farewell letters?"—"Yes. Scott addressed his diary to his wife, and he and the others all wrote farewell letters to their relatives."

I asked Commander Evans whether there was really any question of recovering and bringing back the bodies, and questioned him as to his own and Lady Scott's views on this subject. He said: "We in the expedition who had known these gallant men so intimately were unanimous in our expression of opinion that the bodies should not be disturbed. I know that Lady Scott and Mrs. Wilson entirely support this view."

Scientific Results.

Commander Evans manifestly did not wish to discuss any further the details of the tragedy. In reply to questions on other subjects he said: The geological specimens and the Polar sledge tent and equipment are all being brought home by Lieutenant Pennell in the Terra Nova. With regard to the scientific results of the expedition, a representative committee of members of the expedition has been formed, and each of the scientific staff will work at his own special subject, Dr. Atkinson being responsible for the co-ordination of the whole in the absence of Dr. Simpson, who would have succeeded to the position of chief of the scientific staff had his services not been required by the Government of India.

The Guardian 14th April 1913

TERRA NOVA'S RETURN

London, Friday.

It is stated at Cardiff that the Terra Nova will reach England in August, and that the first United Kingdom port at which she will call will be Cardiff, this being in fulfilment of the undertaking made by Capt. Scott before he sailed for the Antarctic. Lieut Evans is returning home by mail steamer, and is expected back in England in about six weeks

Christchurch, Friday.

The members of the Scott expedition are not in favour of a suggestion that has been made that Australia and New Zealand Governments should charter the Terra Nova, put Lieut Sir Ernest Shackleton in command, and send her to procure the bodies for burial in St. Paul's Cathedral. The members of the expedition say that if they had thought it right to bring the bodies back Commander Evans would have done so.—Reuter

THE WIDOW OF PETTY OFFICER EVANS.

Mrs. Edgar Evans, widow of Petty Officer Evans, yesterday received official notice from the Admiralty of her husband's death in the Antarctic. She has received numerous telegrams and letters of sympathy. In one of his last letters her husband wrote: "Never mind, it will only be another year, and I shall be with you and family."

The Guardian 14th February 1913

"

The bravest are surely those who have the clearest vision of what is before them, glory and danger alike, and yet, notwithstanding, go out to meet it

"

Thucydides

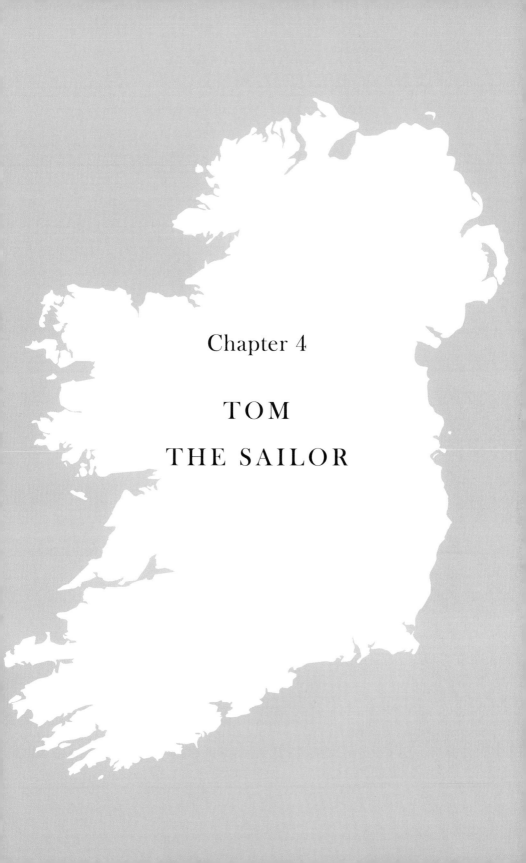

Chapter 4

TOM
THE SAILOR

On 29th December 1913, Sir Ernest Shackleton, by now a famed veteran of Antarctic exploration, announced an ambitious plan to traverse Antarctica from the Weddell Sea to the Ross Sea.[1]

His scheme included the use of two aero sledges with mounted propellers and an airplane at a time when aircraft technology was still in early development and only 10 years since the Wright brothers had first taken to the skies.[2]

Antarctic exploration in 1914, from a geographical standpoint, was still a relatively fledgling enterprise. Undiscovered areas of the continent remained of great interest to the world's scientists and geographers but uppermost in Shackleton's thoughts was the first crossing of Antarctica.

It was proposed that a team of six men would undertake the 1,700-mile crossing led by Shackleton who, when breaking the news, had announced Frank Wild as his second in command.

The plan included the use of two ships and a complement of forty-two men. Holding Amundsen's earlier success up as an example, he proposed taking 120 dogs from Alaska and Siberia to pull the sledges.

One of the ships was to land a twelve-man shore party on the

Sir Ernest Shackleton speaking to a journalist in London on what was a particularly cold New Year's Day. He was, at the time, in the company of Frank Wild:-

'Even Sir Ernest Shackleton is having to abandon his no overcoat, no office fire, all windows open idea. It is not that these two hardened travellers find London's weather uncomfortable. They describe it as dangerous. There is a humidity about the London atmosphere that the Antarctic knows not.

"Just now, I am endeavouring to keep fit for the English winter rather than trouble about training for the Pole trip. There are germs about that make a pet of explorers. In the Antarctic, the only known germ is the germ that creates a fever for wanting to go back there."'

Irish Examiner, 2nd January, 1914

west side of the Weddell Sea before continuing on a mission to trace the southern continuation of Graham Land. Three men would be stationed at winter quarters on the Weddell coast and three of the shore party would explore to the east of the winter quarters, an entirely undiscovered area. The remaining group of six would make the crossing. *"The probability,"* Shackleton said, *"was that the second ship would travel to the Ross Sea side in the summer months in anticipation of meeting the transcontinental group."*

The expedition, it was proposed, would commence in October 1914 and the use of depots was, at this stage, ruled out. Instead a pioneering use of dehydrated food which a team of German scientists were preparing for the journey, would substantially lighten the load and allow for an easier crossing.[3] Eager to tap into to new advancements in technology, Shackleton felt the crossing could be made without the aid of a supporting party and could be completed over the course of five months.

Within days of the announcement, Shackleton was expressing concerns about his plans.[4] Critics considered his ambitions to be too daring and revolutionary. Use of an airplane would not, on this occasion, materialise for a man

whose thinking was ahead of his time and
by the level of technology that had not yet (
visions.

Ever the optimist, Shackleton had appe
flight technology of the era but, with only crude versions available
and without a testing environment that could mimic Antarctic conditions, the idea proved to be overambitious. It was, though, a con-
cept he would later rekindle by taking a plane, an *Avro Baby*, on his
final expedition aboard *Quest* but that, too, was destined never to
get off the ground owing to a number of missing parts.

For the landing at the Weddell Sea side (of Antarctica), from
which the crossing attempt would be made, Shackleton purchased
a ship named *Polaris* and renamed her *Endurance*. The use of two
ships remained vital to Shackleton's plans and the *SY Aurora* would
carry the party whose task, it was later decided, would be to lay supply depots from the Ross Sea side of the continent in preparation for
the journey of Shackleton's team on the opposite side.

His first choices to crew *Endurance,* announced in February
1914, were a number of polar veterans, among them were Lieutenant
Aeneas MacIntosh, who was to head up the *Aurora* crew, and Alf
Cheetham, another Antarctic veteran, who was recruited as third officer for the *Endurance*. At the same time, it was also announced
that Captain John King Davis, another member with polar experience who had served with Shackleton aboard *Nimrod*, would captain
the *Endurance*.[5] It was a position he later declined in May 1914 after
accepting a Commonwealth role offered to him by the Australian
government. His replacement would be a New Zealander, a Royal
Navy Reservist, Frank Worsley.[6]

Discussions were also taking place between the Admiralty and

...kleton, who was seeking their permission to recruit men from the navy who had taken part in Scott's expedition.

The reputation of one navy man, in particular, had not been lost on Shackleton. The selection of Tom Crean - who, a year before, had received his Albert Medal after his heroic life-saving solo march - would have been seen as a high priority for Shackleton but there was a rival explorer seeking the services of the Kerryman.[7]

The previous year, in October 1913, it had also been reported that Joseph Foster Stackhouse was to lead a British Antarctic Expedition and his plans were to head south on 1st August 1914.[8]

Responding to the question, *"What makes the best explorers?"*, put forward by a London Daily News journalist in January 1914, Foster Stackhouse staked his claim:

"There is a tendency for polar explorers to get melancholia. The utter isolation, the monotonous whiteness of everything, the oppressive silence will soon get on a man's nerves unless he is the right type. The long winter night is a very severe test, too. No one who has not known what it is like to live for five months without a glimpse of daylight or the sun can have any conception of the nervous strain of an Antarctic winter. Only men of exactly the right temperament can stand it.

The tendency is to go mad. Many men with the wrong temperament would go mad. Imagine what it is like to go out into the darkness day after day, and to hear no sound except perhaps the ticking of your watch. The silence is uncanny. There is no other silence like it. In the most desolate country, you may hear the cries of birds or animals but in the Antarctic winter there is nothing. It's this appalling silence that has made several polar workers give way to melancholia. Anyone who reads Captain Scott's diaries will notice how careful he was in selecting his polar party and how grateful he was to them for being unendingly cheerful in the most desperate positions. They joked when they were starving and knew they had no chance to get through.

That is the type of man you want; the man who will make a joke when there is no fuel left and only one biscuit each and the next depot is thirty miles away. The habitual humourist who cannot help seeing the bright and amusing side of things is invaluable in polar work. When things go wrong, you must have men who will laugh and put them right, not men who will accept the situation and do nothing."

He'd described Crean to a tee and Foster Stackhouse then took the opportunity to single him out adding:

"One of the finest feats in Scott's Expedition was Crean's walk of thirty-five miles to get help for Commander Evans. He walked along all those miles at a stretch, though ten miles of such a walk would have sent hundreds of men clean out of their minds. But Crean is an Irishman with an incorrigible sense of humour and it was this that carried him through. There should be an Irishman in every expedition."[9]

It was announced as late as 4th May 1914 that Foster Stackhouse, a close friend of Captain Scott who had helped raise finances for the ill-fated *Terra Nova* expedition, was clearly planning on taking Tom Crean as his boatswain and was also a prospective buyer for *Polaris,* but he withdrew from the sale believing the ship was not up to the task.

Finding himself in the position of being headhunted, Crean's decision was made easier when Foster Stackhouse's mission to chart the Antarctic coastline of King Edward's Land to Graham Land on the British National Antarctic Expedition was postponed until 1915.

The ship Foster Stackhouse eventually secured for the 1915 expedition was *Discovery,* a vessel Crean knew well after his maiden voyage with Scott to Antarctica in 1901. What influenced Crean to join Shackleton's crew aboard *Endurance* is not known but it appears he was eager to return to Antarctica and waiting a further year was not an option. Foster Stackhouse's expedition would later grow more ambitious and, on 22nd June 1914, it was announced that the proposed journey would now be a "*seven-year cruise*" of exploration.[10]

Crean, perhaps with an assurance from Shackleton that he would be a member of the six-man crossing party and not wishing to commit to a seven-year absence, made his decision to join Shackleton. His appointment to the expedition was formally announced on the same day.[11] Crean's inclusion in the team to make the crossing, along with Wild, Hurley, Marston, Macklin and Shackleton himself, was later referred to in a letter Shackleton wrote while *Endurance* was moored in Buenos Aires.[12]

Earlier, in December 1913, before Shackleton's announcement and when it appeared the schedule of the two expeditions may clash, Foster Stackhouse and Shackleton discussed the possibility of crossover in one another's aims. They concluded that both expeditions could co-exist without an overlapping of their prospective missions.[13]

It is likely, in their meeting, that the subject of Tom Crean was on the agenda and it's an interesting thought to imagine the two expedition leaders asserting their rights over the recruitment of the Annascaul man.

Sadly, the rescheduling of the proposed *Discovery* expedition was a date Foster Stackhouse himself would never meet. On 7th May

1915, the *Lusitania,* for a short time the largest passenger ship in the world, was torpedoed by a German U-Boat eleven miles off the coast of Kinsale with the loss of 1,198 lives. Among the dead was Joseph Foster Stackhouse, who was sailing back to England after visiting the USA on what had been a successful fundraising trip for the forthcoming expedition.

One account of a survivor, Lieutenant Frederic Lasseter, an infantryman who'd been wounded in Flanders, recalled Foster Stackhouse fastening his own lifebelt to a little girl and hurriedly assisting women into lifeboats. Stackhouse told Lasseter to look for his mother.

Joseph Foster Stackhouse

When the Lasseters returned, Stackhouse told the young officer: *"You'd better jump."*

Mr. J. Foster Stackhouse

Commander of the

British Antarctic Expedition 1914

in ordering large supplies of Oxo for his Expedition writes :

I herewith enclose you order for Oxo for use on the above Expedition.

I may mention that I have gone very exhaustively into the question of concentrated beef foods, using not only my own knowledge of the matter, but being assisted by published results of other Antarctic Explorers. These having proved beyond doubt that Oxo is the best article of its kind, I have decided to rely on it exclusively.

Yours faithfully,

J. FOSTER STACKHOUSE.

"The Discovery,"
From a Sketch by Mr. J. F. Stackhouse

The selection of Oxo by Mr. Stackhouse confirms the experience of other well-known explorers and of hundreds of Hospitals and Institutions who have made diet a study and constantly use Oxo. They have learnt the value of the Oxo guarantee—

"the ONLY British Fluid Beef that gets all its beef from ITS OWN CATTLE "—

a guarantee which ensures unique body-building properties, standardisation and absolute purity.

Unlike beef tea, Oxo is prepared by scientific processes which provide in an assimilable form the all-important nourishing properties of beef as well as the extractives which stimulate and promote digestion.

All who value health and stamina should include Oxo in their diet. It builds up strength and nourishes the system without taxing the digestion.

OXO, Thames House, London, E.C.

ANTARCTIC EXPLORATION.

AN ELEMENTARY SCHOOL'S HELP.

Mr. George Marston, who was a member of Sir Ernest Shackleton's last Antarctic expedition and is going out with him again on his next, gave an address last night at Blackley. His visit was an honour conferred at the request of Sir Ernest Shackleton on the Blackley Municipal School, which arranged a concert in aid of the expedition. The proceeds are to be devoted to the purchase of a sledge and sleeping suits, and Sir Ernest has promised that, if possible, the sledge, when it has served its purpose on the Polar ice, shall be returned to the school.

Mr. Marston was regarded with something like veneration by the boys and girls who made up a considerable part of the crowded audience at the concert. He had brought with him some beautiful photographic lantern pictures, and he told a plain story of the life and work of Arctic explorers. The penguins, as usual, had an honoured place both in the story and in the pictures. They interested the audience as much as they seemed to interest the explorer. He paid quite a high tribute to the companionable qualities of these unconsciously humorous creatures. Members of the expedition, he said, used to enjoy sitting among them, and valued their visits to the ship so highly that they tied up the dogs, who would otherwise have molested them. Their company he prescribed as an infallible cure for bad humours. No man however ill his temper, could watch them for long without laughing himself into a more amiable mood.

Of the forthcoming expedition Mr. Marston said nothing except, incidentally, that it would rely for transport over the ice mainly upon dogs. The ponies that were used on the last expedition were, he said, very sturdy and willing, but they were too heavy and too slow. Men suffered from the same disabilities. Dogs scored over them both.

Eleven van loads of Sir Ernest Shackleton's Antarctic expedition dogs crossing London Bridge on their way to Spratt's Quarantine Kennels at Beddington, where a Spratt's dog cake diet will put them in condition for their arduous work on the Southern ice-fields. Insets show three types of the dogs.

DOGS THAT MAY HELP TO MAKE HISTORY.

SIR E. SHACKLETON'S NINETY-NINE "HUSKIES" NOW IN QUARANTINE.

Sir Ernest Shackleton's Dogs, which arrived in London from Canada last Tuesday week (July 14th), have taken kindly to civilisation; but their stay in England is quickly drawing to a close, for on Wednesday next (July 29th) the Trans-Antarctic expedition ship, the Endurance, sails from West India Docks for Buenos Aires. They are big-hearted lovable creatures, these ninety-nine happy dogs that know not their fate, but as the Canadian teamster, who accompanied them from Winnipeg, remarked to a reporter on their arrival, "they just fight like blazes when they get together, unless they are in the teams of five in which they work."

Sleighing and hauling fish is their chief use in Canada, and each is capable of drawing a load of at least one hundred pounds. They can travel forty miles a day, if necessary.

In their native homes away out in the North West Territory and along the shores of the Hudson Bay, where half their ancestry was composed of wolves, they have lived mainly on fish, but now that they are at Spratt's Quarantine Kennels at Beddington biscuits are substituted, and the remarkable manner in which they are flourishing during this spell of hot weather while being used to intense cold, speaks well for the change of diet. These half-savage team-dogs had never tasted a biscuit until they started on the voyage from Montreal to London, but they consumed two thousand pounds of Spratt's "Meat Fibrine" Dog Cakes by the time they arrived, and are now confirmed biscuit eaters. That they should have taken so readily to their new food is indeed most fortunate, for much more depends on this than one would imagine. The late Captain Scott admitted that his failure to reach the Pole on his 1901 expedition in the "Discovery" was due to the fact that he substituted stockfish for biscuits as food for the dogs which accompanied him on his final dash. In his report appear the following remarks: "It would be unprofitable, as well as dismal, to give a close history of the further career of our wretched Dog Team. They failed us almost immediately after we had formed such high hopes of travelling a long distance. The failure was certainly due to the Stockfish."

There is, however, no fear of anything of this sort happening in connection with the Trans-Antarctic Expedition, for Sir Ernest Shackleton has made ample provision for feeding his dogs on biscuits, the supply of Spratt's Dog Cakes on board the Endurance being sufficient to last throughout the Expedition.

The dogs answer promptly to their names—Blackey, Collar, Noble, Captain, Nero, Colonel, Chimo, etc.

Of the ninety-nine, whose ages range from one to six years, 60 are unusually large, the remainder being younger and somewhat smaller. In many of them the features of the St. Bernard, Newfoundland and German Wolfhound are very pronounced, but they are all half-breeds. "Fox" is a very pretty dog, if not the prettiest of the pack. A remarkable clever and well-trained animal, he is one of the team-leaders, although but a year old. "Light," an all-grey dog of the Prairie Wolf type, is another of the team leaders. He is the champion of them all, the best worker and the fiercest fighter.

Irish Independent 22nd July 1914

OFF TO THE SOUTH

SHACKLETON CHOOSES MEN

(Published in "The Times" this Morning)

LONDON.

Captain Worsley, of New Zealand, has been appointed to command Sir Ernest Shackleton's exploration ship Endeavour.

Petty-officer Thomas Crean, who rescued Commander E. R. G. Evans, of Scott's expedition, and was a member of the party that discovered the dead bodies of Captain Scott and his companions, is going with the shore staff.

The Times 23rd June 1914

ANTARCTIC EXPEDITION, 1914.

COLONIES INVITED TO SUPPLY SCIENTIFIC MEMBERS.

Mr. J. Foster Stackhouse, the leader of the British Antarctic Expedition of 1914, has decided, the Central News understands, to give his expedition an Imperial character by inviting each of the Dominions to send representatives on the scientific staff. He has invited Australia and New Zealand to provide two geologists, South Africa a meteorologist, and Canada a physicist. Mr. Stackhouse has received some thousands of applications from men eager to join the expedition.

The Guardian
20th December 1913

Views of Mr. Stackhouse.

Mr. J. Foster Stackhouse, leader, of the British Antarctic Expedition, 1914, interviewed by a Central News representative, said it was quite true to say that there was no rivalry between his own expedition and that of Sir Ernest Shackleton. He and Sir Ernest had, in fact, talked over their plans with a view to avoid any overlapping in their respective spheres of exploration. Sir Ernest Shackleton had formulated a bold scheme, and if completely carried out would add greatly to the world's knowledge of the Antarctic. If he (Mr. Stackhouse) succeeded in exploring King Edward VII.'s Land and the base of the Graham Peninsula, and Shackleton were successful in charting the coast from his base towards the Larsen Sea, there would be little left to do in the western quadrants.

Freeman Journal
30th December 1913

94

LATEST ARRANGEMENTS

(P. A. Foreign Special).

London, Monday Night.

The Press Association understands that rapid progress is being made in the arrangement of the final details for the Imperial Transantarctic Expedition. Sir Ernest Shackleton has appointed Captain F. A. Worsley, lieutenant R.N.R., to the command of his new ship Endurance, and he will al. be in charge of the hydrographical work of the expedition. Capt. Worsley has had 26 years at sea, eight years in sailing ships, eight years in the New Zealand Government marine service, and six years in the Allan Line until his appointment. He was the first officer of the Alsatian. He has had large experience of ice work.

Other new appointments to Sir Edward's staff are Mr H. E. Wild, brother of Mr Frank Wild, second in command of the expedition, to the shore staff, and Mr Tom Crean, who was on two Scott expeditions and received the Albert medal for rescuing Commander Evans. He will also join the shore staff.

One hundred and five dogs specially selected by the Hudson Bay Company from trading post teams in Arctic Canada are leaving Montreal for Liverpool in a few days. Ten of these will be brought to London for inspection, while the remainder will go by direct steamer to Buenos Ayres to avoid a slow journey through the tropics.

Sir Ernest's new ship Endurance, intended for the Weddell Sea side of the expedition, is practically ready for sea. The hut for the winter quarters has been completed, and is on board, while the biological and dredging gear will be fitted next week. All stores are being shipped to a special shed in the docks. It has now been arranged that after reaching Buenos Ayres the Endurance will go to the Falkland Islands and thence to Deception Island, in the South Shetlands, in the Antarctic, where she will ship 100 tons of coals. Arrangements have been concluded with Norwegian whalers so that the ship shall eventually enter the Weddell Sea with full bunkers.

The Aurora, which is intended for the Ross Sea base, will be formally taken over by Sir Ernest Shackleton in August. Arrangements are now being made for her staff, and the ship will leave Hobart in November.

Irish Examiner
23rd June 1914

Lasseter's final recollection before he leapt from the sinking vessel was hearing others urging Stackhouse to board one of the lifeboats. He refused, stating: *"There are others that must go first."*

From the safety of the lifeboat, Lasseter and his mother looked on helplessly as the sturdy figure of his friend and a hero, Foster Stackhouse, still without a lifebelt, stood calmly on the stern with his arms folded moments before the ship sank.[14] His body was later recovered and he was buried in Cork in a Quaker graveyard.

Tom Crean's final posting, before heading south once more, was between 23rd January and 24th May 1914 aboard the Admiralty yacht, *HMS Enchantress*.[15] Before the outbreak of the First World War, the vessel had been a favoured means of travel for the First Lord of the Admiralty, Winston Churchill, who used it to tour and inspect naval bases and dockyards, and to make visits abroad. Indeed records reveal that both Crean and Churchill were aboard the vessel at the same time in February 1914.[16]

On 25th May 1914, Crean's naval service would, as it had on two previous occasions, be ledgered to *HMS President* for his third journey to Antarctica.[17]

Shackleton and Crean had already been acquainted some thirteen years earlier while serving under Scott on the *Discovery* expedition. While *Discovery* had been the launch pad for both men's Antarctic careers, it was also the beginning of a strained relationship Shackleton had with Scott, having been ordered home early on health grounds much to his dismay.

Crean, now a Chief Petty Officer and an Antarctic veteran, was to act as Shackleton's second officer and he was placed in charge of sledges.

On 16th July, *Endurance,* berthed at Millwall Docks, was visited by Queen Alexandra and members of her family, where Shackleton presented the Royal party to the officers of the expedition. Insisting on seeing every nook and cranny of the vessel, Queen Alexandra was accompanied down to the galley where she put a number of questions to the cook. At a time when social sensitivities were rarely a consideration, the Queen remarked: *"it was a very little galley... it was perhaps fortunate that he was a small man."*[18]

Interestingly, a journalist from The Guardian, who had visited the newly-built ship for a tour two days earlier, reported that the ship carried *"two ordinary boats, a whaler and a motor launch."*[19] It is a reference to a fourth boat, the motor launch, that intrigues here as there appears to be no further mention of the vessel in the drama that would later unfold.

Endurance left her berth at the West India Dock on 1st August 1914 and headed for Plymouth before sailing on to South America. Shackleton was at the helm and the Manchester Guardian reported that *"alongside the skipper and at the wheel was a hero - Petty Officer Crean, the man who saved Commander Evan's life."*[20]

The expedition had a quiet send-off, which was not surprising given the tensions of the time; Britain officially declared war with Germany the following day. At the dock gate, the Scottish Piper, McPherson,[21] was welcomed aboard and proceeded to pace the decks playing the ship out to sea en route to Plymouth. The newspaper reported:

"the piper struck up 'The Wearing O' The Green' as there are both Ulstermen and Nationalists aboard and they look forward to keeping themselves warm with argument in the long nights in winter quarters."[22]

Shackleton remained in Britain and set sail to join the expedition on 18th September aboard a steamer to Buenos Aires, with a

The rations were complete on board with the exception of the sledge rations. Sir Ernest told a representative on board the Endurance, that the rations have been prepared under advice from War Office experts. The whole ration will consist of lard, bovril powder, glidine, (a plant based protein concentrate), cane sugar and oatmeal. This will be kept in cold storage and will be taken morning and night. In the daytime, the finest mixture of nuts with oil and powdered milk will form the food on the march. Very little tea will be taken during sledging operations.

Morning refreshments will be milk, lunch, tea and, at night, Bovril. They also had gelatine and lime juice capsules produced by a new method by War Office experts, which had the effect of concentrating it by 10 times in vacuo. Heat was prevented from killing it and it was anti-scurvy.

cargo carrying the dogs and the motor sledges. From Argentina, the *Endurance* set sail on 26th October 1914, en route to South Georgia. After a month-long stay, the ship left Grytviken heading towards its Antarctic destination on 5th December 1914.

It became apparent within days that the mission to reach the Weddell Sea landing point would be fraught with difficulties and the pack ice hampered the ship's progress throughout their journey. By 14th February 1915, when the ice had become an impenetrable barrier, the crew attempted to break her free, leaving the ship to use picks and saws to cut through the ice and allow further progress. *Endurance* and her crew had become slaves to the drifting ice that gripped her and, for the following months, the crew could do little in their battle to free her from the ice.

To maintain morale and physical fitness, the crew would take strolls and, on occasion, they would take to the polar football pitch where Crean employed a controversial tactic to prevent the opposing side from scoring. Now a seasoned polar player after his performances during the Terra Nova expedition, if Crean thought an opposing player might get the better of him, he'd grab him, wrestle him to the ground and sit on him until the danger had passed.[23] His methods rendered the opposing side a man short, while his own team took full advantage at the other end of the pitch.

By now, it had become clear that any efforts to free *Endurance* from the ice had become a futile exercise and, finally, on 27th October 1915, Shackleton gave the order to abandon ship.

All useful provisions were removed, including the aero sledges designed by Orde Lees which had proved to be a disaster, constantly breaking down and having to be man-hauled. Shackleton, the leader who championed innovations of the era (he had taken a motor car on his previous expedition aboard *Nimrod*), was let down by invention once again and the crew were glad to see the back of them. Their use now was limited to the plywood body that made up their structure.

The ambitions of the expedition now lay in tatters, and their mission had become a race for survival. In the days before instant communication for emergency assistance, the group of twenty-eight men faced an uncertain future. For three days, the party camped on the ice close to the ship and the time was used to retrieve more supplies and the three lifeboats from the doomed vessel. There was, by now, little choice but to embark upon a march in

The rations continued...

In the event of an emergency, they had an appliance whereby boiling liquid could be produced anywhere in 25 seconds...

The liquid was placed in a cartridge and then into a tube and then the cartridge is set on fire. The Primus stove would still be used but about forty cartridges would be taken on each journey in case of a blizzard or other emergency.

Antarctic Expedition. (1914, September 30). Leader (Orange, NSW: 1912-1922), p.4. http:// nla.gov.au/nla.news-article117879859

the hope of taking to the open sea if there was to be any hope of the group's survival.

Attempting to haul two of the ship's lifeboats, the *James Caird* and the *Dudley Docker*, the group made little progress and were further hampered by the drifting ice pack they were travelling upon. After making barely four miles, they made camp within sight of the *Endurance* on 1st November 1915. It was christened *Ocean Camp*.

If ever the phrase 'two steps forward, one step back' applied in the literal sense, it was now; efforts to travel in the right direction would be made futile by the direction of an uncontrollable ice pack that would prevent them launching the boats and reaching salvation.

On 23rd December, due to warmer conditions giving rise to soft snow in the camp, it became necessary to haul the boats on a second march to firmer ground.

Frustrations were creeping in when there appeared little chance of the group reaching safety. Hauling the boats over uneven ground was proving difficult and three days after leaving *Ocean Camp*, the ship's carpenter, Harry McNish, refused to carry on. His anger had been further fuelled by Shackleton's orders to kill the weakest animals after the party had abandoned the ship. Among those killed was McNish's cat, Chippy.

McNish argued that, because Ship's Articles (the contract by which crew members agree to conditions, payment and the authority of a leader) were no longer relevant, he was no longer subject to orders from his expedition leader. Shackleton acted quickly to admonish the rebellious McNish and the group continued. It was an incident McNish later lived to regret and recognition for what would become his vital role in this tale was denied him.

On 29th December 1915, two months after abandoning ship, the group erected their tents to set up what Shackleton would call *Patience Camp*, still drifting north on the ice. It would become their home for the next three months. Throughout their time on *Patience Camp*, frequent forays back to their previous ice settlement, *Ocean Camp*, became necessary as supplies ran low. Food and other resources had been left there in order to lighten the sledges when they had been forced to leave.

In mid-January 1916, a decision was made to shoot thirty-five of the dogs. It was clear that they could never be taken aboard the lifeboats and their voracious appetites, at a time when seals were in short supply, proved too excessive with twenty-eight men to feed. Although it was the right decision, it was made harder by the bonds that had been formed among the crew and their animal charges. Animal lovers like Crean, who had played foster father to four puppies born to Sally, one of the dogs he had been put in charge of, found the killings distressing yet understood that survival of the crew was the greater priority.

On 12th February 1916, a group of eighteen men led by Crean and Frank Hurley as pathfinders, returned again to their former camp to recover the remaining lifeboat, the *Stancomb Wills*.

Thousands of miles away, in warmer climes, a concerned public were becoming anxious about the crew they had heard nothing of since their departure almost two years earlier. One reporter recalled the muted departure at West India Docks in 1914 and remembered the tiny group of Eastenders there to bid farewell to *Endurance*:

"I remember that Crean, that magnificent veteran in polar exploration, showed the visitors all over the marvellously compact and ingenious quarters and storerooms, where there was not an inch of space wasted. From Tilbury pier, we watched the sturdy

*wooden ship fading into the mist and caught a last glimpse of
Shackleton staring towards London."*[24]

It read almost like an obituary, as if forewarning the public of a
dark update such as happened in 1912 with Scott's expedition.

Prospects for the twenty-eight men camped on the ice certainly
looked bleak as they contemplated their next move in the fight for
survival.

The remaining dogs were shot on 2nd April and their meat provided additional rations for the men.

On 8th April 1916, the floe on which they'd pitched their camp
split. Their time at *Patience Camp* had come to an end and, after another precarious night camping on a dangerously small ice floe barely
one hundred feet long, all three lifeboats were forced to launch on 9th
April 1916.

The original plan was to head for Deception Island and, between
them, the boats carried twenty-eight men. Skippering the boats, as they
sought a means of reaching civilisation and salvation, were the three
men who would play the pivotal roles in the extraordinary tale of rescue
and survival that lay ahead. Expedition leader Ernest Shackleton com-
manded the *James Caird*, largest of the three lifeboats. Frank Worsley, Captain of the *Endurance*, took charge of the *Dudley Docker*, and
skippering duty of the smallest of the boats, the *Stancomb Wills*, was
delegated to Tom Crean.

After a few hours at the oars, the flotilla of lifeboats was at the
mercy of an inrush of pack ice rolling violently in, the waves now heading in their direction. Frank Hurley, aboard the *James Caird* noted:

*"Tossing, plunging and grinding, the fearsome menace swept
after us with hellish speed and, though we pulled with all our*

might, we could not draw away. The ice-laden surge was only one hundred yards behind and tongues of ice were flicking out ahead of it. One of these reached to within a few yards of the Stancomb Wills which was bringing up the rear end; disaster was only averted by the greatest exertion of her crew and Crean's skillful piloting."

After an arduous thirty-six hours at the oars, the crews pitched up on a large floe-berg for a much-needed rest and an opportunity to enjoy hot food. On 11th April, after waiting hours for the heavy sea swells to die down, the boats, once again, entered the narrow sea lanes that opened up between the ice floes. Another hard day's navigation followed and, again on 12th April, they found an overnight home on an ice floe. Crean, Shackleton and Worsley remained in the boats to prevent potential damage from the drifting floes surrounding them. On 13th April, they made clear of the ice and started to make good progress. By this stage, Shackleton had a change of plan and Elephant Island was to be their destination.

Often overshadowed by the events thereafter, the journey that led them to Elephant Island presented all three boats with grave dangers. The seas around them threatened to swallow them up, particularly in the dead of night when obstacles such as glaciers were an ever-present danger. Tom Crean's task proved most difficult, given that the boat he skippered was the smallest and most vulnerable.

In the distance on 14th April, they spotted Elephant Island. Due to strong gales, it was decided that the *James Caird* take the *Stancomb Wills* in tow as two of the smaller boat's crew, Hudson and Blackborrow, were suffering from severe frostbite.

On 15th April, Shackleton climbed into the *Stancomb Wills* and navigated the small boat through an opening in the reef onto a stone beach. Here, they set up camp on a small inlet on the desolate, uninhabited Elephant Island.

Perce Blackborrow, at 18-years-old, the youngest member of the expedition, had the honour of being the first man to set foot on Elephant Island. Blackborrow had earlier been smuggled aboard *Endurance* by two other crew members, William Bakewell and Walter How, before she set sail from Buenos Aires, yet had since proved his worth after being discovered hidden in a locker. It was, though, a painful affair for the young Welsh stowaway, as he fell from the side of the boat into the freezing waters and had to be carried to shore owing to his severely frostbitten feet.

Shackleton later described the elated experience of reaching solid land after eighteen months on the ice, telling how the men, after landing on the beach, *"gloated over pebbles like misers over gold."*[25]

On closer inspection, their landing place presented too many dangers for a lengthy stay and the following morning, 16th April, it was decided that Wild and a four-man crew, including Tom Crean, would take to the *Stancomb Wills* and look for a more suitable place to make camp. They returned later in the day with the news that a place had been found. On 17th April, early in the morning and in heavy sea conditions, they took to the boats once again and made their way seven miles along the coast.

Perilously sailing close to the rocky shoreline, all three boats were at the mercy of the raging seas around them until two of the boats, the *James Caird* and the *Stancomb Wills*, reached calmer waters with the safer beach now visible. The *Stancomb Wills* was first to land followed by the *James Caird*. The strain was now beginning to show after a terrifying ordeal that left the crews soaked, shaken and desperate for rest. Lewis Rickinson, who had been originally hired as the Chief Engineer for *Endurance*, suffered a mild heart attack, yet, still, despite his suffering, laboured on with the rest of the men unloading provisions from the boats onto the beach. Within half an hour, the *Dudley Docker*, to the relief of those already ashore, was spotted and broke through the surf to land safely.

Their landing site was christened Point Wild after its discoverer Frank Wild, Shackleton's deputy, and it was soon decided that more extreme risks had to be undertaken if they were to have any chance of survival.

The *Dudley Docker* and the *Stancomb Wills* lifeboats were up-turned and laid side by side to help provide shelter for most of the group, who would have to remain on the island if there was to be any hope of rescue. The largest of the three boats, the *James Caird*, was cleverly adapted by McNish, the carpenter, in the hope it would resist the ravages of the treacherous Southern Ocean - a sea crossing that would enter the history books as the most daring and ambitious ma-rine rescue of all time.

On 24th April 1916, six men took to the *James Caird* as it em-barked upon what would be a torturous journey to South Georgia.

Referring to the launch, Frank Wild stated:

"It was only by a hair's breadth that, at the start, the boat es-caped being smashed up. She had no ballast and, when she was launched broadside-on, there was a nasty sea running inshore. Crean saved her by fending her off with an oar just at the right moment and, fortunately, the wind was off the land and blew her out once she was afloat."[26]

Shackleton's style of leadership saw him selflessly include McNish, who had earlier questioned his leadership. John Vincent, who had been demoted from *Boatswain* to *Able Seaman* after an altercation with Orde-Lees, was also included.

The three Irishmen aboard were oblivious to events taking place in their homeland the very same day that they launched their boat. Ten thousand miles away in Ireland, men and women had taken to the streets and were prepared to lay down their lives in pursuit of freedom from British rule. The *Easter Rising* (Éirí Amach na Cásca) had begun, and it would later give rise to the birth of an independent nation, the Republic of Ireland.

Maintaining good morale was imperative for the main body of men left at Elephant Island under the stewardship of Shackleton's second in command, Frank Wild. Making up the sixth member of the crew and, along with Tom Crean and Ernest Shackleton, one of the three Irishmen aboard, was Timothy McCarthy, a Cork-born sailor whose skills and calm character had left a great impression on Shackleton. Tom Crean took over cooking duties on a single-burner Primus stove, crouching over it in the most difficult of small spaces in conditions that made cooking almost impossible. Struggling to serve up the rations of hoosh with huge waves crashing into and over the small lifeboat, clumps of reindeer hairs from their drenched sleeping bags were falling into the pot providing the six men with an unwelcome addition to their meal.

For Crean, it is hard to imagine that a man's spirit in these conditions could do anything other than plummet to the lowest depths. The crew were faced with the near-certainty that their time on earth was up and their impending demise would go unreported. They would be lost to the elements and leave without goodbyes to loved ones. Their inadequate, torn clothing, soaked in freezing salt water, permanently shrouded their bodies. Just to relieve themselves, men had to negotiate their rear ends over the frozen sides of a boat surrounded by gigantic waves. Astonishingly, through all of this, Tom Crean kept spirits afloat with song, humour and wit.

Frank Worsley captured the atmosphere best, as he later recalled in his book the banter between Crean and Shackleton:

"It was partly chaff and partly a comic revolt against the conditions. Tom Crean had been so long and done so much with Sir Ernest that he had become a privileged retainer. As these two watchmates turned in, a kind of wordless, rumbling, muttering, growling noise could be heard issuing from the dark and gloomy lair in the bows, sometimes at things in general and sometimes at nothing at all. At times, they were so full of quaint conceit, and Crean's remarks were so Irish that I ran the risk of explosion by suppressed laughter.

Shackleton: "Go to sleep, Crean, and don't be clucking like an old hen."

Crean: "Boss, I can't eat those old reindeer hairs. I'll have an inside on me like a billy goat's neck. Let's give 'em to the skipper and McCarthy. They never know what they're eating."

Perhaps this camaraderie and the ability to focus minds elsewhere, away from the dangers that surround people in a such a crisis, is what set men such as Crean, Shackleton and Worsley apart. It is a trait that is understated and forgotten when history books concentrate more on the physical feats of human endurance in this great tale of survival.

Through the imminent dangers of the storms that, at any time, could spell the end for them, calmness was typified by Tom Crean who, on the rare occasions that a break in the weather allowed, could be heard singing away whilst keeping watch, as Worsley later recalled:

"In some of the few fine watches, Crean made noises at the helm that we surmised represented 'The Wearin' o' the Green.' Another series of sounds, however, completely baffled us."

Throughout their journey, the Southern Ocean *"maintained its evil winter reputation,"* as Shackleton would later recall.

Thick sections of ice were continually forming on the sides of the boat and the rudder. Tirelessly, the men worked day and night, hacking it away and bailing water from the boat.

All the time, the six men retained their spirits in an effort to minimise what increasingly appeared to be a hopeless mission. At a time midway through their journey, when they had been forced to jettison much of the equipment owing to the increased weight of ice that relentlessly bonded to every part of the vessel, Shackleton, speaking to reporters after their ordeal was over, said: *"I wish to record the cheerful attitude of my companions."* The *James Caird* was by now, though, dangerously close to becoming nothing more than a floating coffin.

Tossed around in the huge swells that kept the men frantically bailing water from the bottom of their boat and with Vincent's condition worsening, making a safe landing had become a matter of the greatest urgency. Fifteen days into their journey, all of the group were suffering with an extreme thirst, having depleted their water reserves, and all had become severely weakened by the ravages of the journey. The bitterly cold winds and snowstorms that battered into the small craft had taken their toll on the crew and each man was victim to frostbite. Worsley metaphorically described the effects on himself and Crean:

"Our hands had become awful objects to look upon. Crean's and mine, in addition to being almost black with grime, blubber and soot, were ornamented with recent frostbite and burns from the Primus. Each successive frostbite on a finger was marked by a ring where the skin had peeled up to, so that we could count our frostbites by the rings after the method a woodman uses when telling the age of a tree."

On 9th May, they spotted South Georgia. Their relief was indescribable, yet still great dangers persisted.

Hurricane conditions restricted their plan to land near the inhabited side of the island and they waited offshore before a change in the weather allowed them a way in. The following day, after setting a reefed sail to improve their chances, they landed at dusk in a small cove on the desolate side of the island they had departed from with high hopes a year and a half earlier.

How they made it defies belief on all counts. The difficulties of navigation in perilous seas that offered them no quarter proved a task that only the most skilled of navigators could have achieved. Frank Worsley, the skipper, was that man.

Two of the crew, McNish and Vincent, were so weakened by the ordeal they could barely walk. Not only had the mettle of Tom Crean proved invaluable, his power to inspire others when all seemed lost had also helped them to this point - albeit with a dismal outlook for their future survival.

> "
>
> *Faith is taking the first step even when you don't see the whole staircase*
>
> "
>
> **Martin Luther King, Jr**

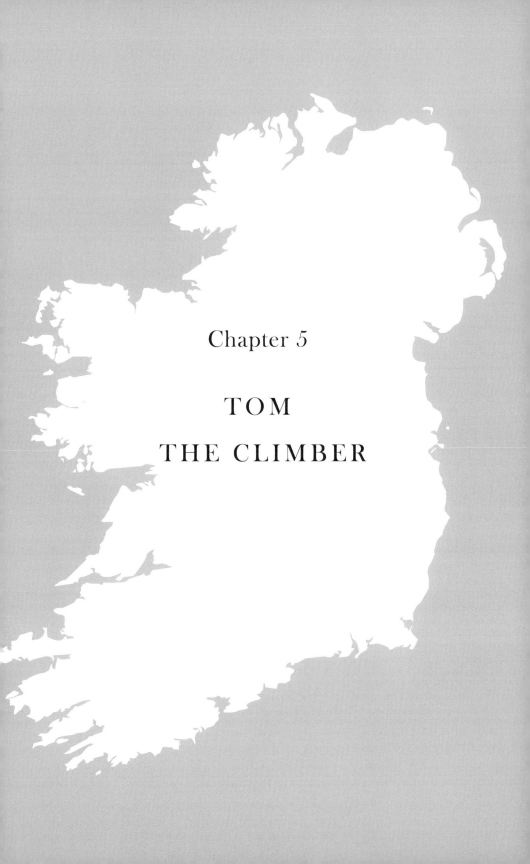

Chapter 5

TOM
THE CLIMBER

Left battered and damaged by the journey, it became clear that the *James Caird* could not survive an attempt to make the sea journey to the whaling station on the opposite side of the island. After five days' rest, the boat did, however, make one final short journey on 15th May to a safer shingle beach on King Haakon Bay. There, the men continued their recuperation in what became known as *Peggoty Camp* (a Dickensian reference to the upturned *James Caird* lifeboat that became their refuge). After a further four-day rest, in the early hours of 19th May 1916, the still exhausted Shackleton, Crean and Worsley set off by the light of the moon to cross the uncharted peaks and ridges of South Georgia where ice chasms were an ever-present danger. McNish, the carpenter who had earlier rebelled and would later be denied a Polar Medal, had driven sixteen two-inch brass screws, eight for each foot, point down into their boots for traction. The three men in their torn, inadequate clothing, carried a small Primus stove, three days' rations and travelled without sleeping bags as they embarked.

All three were roped together with Shackleton in the lead, Worsley navigating and Tom Crean providing the physical backbone of this triumvirate of history-makers. After several navigational errors, the

Expedition members and their falls - an explanation.

Sir Ernest Shackleton, lecturing at Leeds on his experiences in the Antarctic, related an amusing story:

"When anyone fell through the ice", he said, "we pulled him out again. I was rather concerned for the first man who fell in and gave him rum to bring him round. Then eight men fell through the ice in quick succession. I gave the ninth man cocoa and the accidents ceased."

In the Papers, 1921, The Argus, Melbourne, Vic: 1848-1957, p.7.

three had to retrace their steps, finding themselves back where they had been several hours earlier, fatigued and frostbitten. Time was against them and further risks had to be undertaken if they were to reach the safe haven of the whaling community at Stromness.

Night was again falling and the three men faced a dilemma as they encountered a steep slope that would provide a huge barrier to their progress unless they took drastic action. There was a danger they would freeze to death at the high altitude and, so, with nothing to lose and the lives of their twenty-five companions in their hands, they took a risk; they formed a human sled with their ropes, sat astride one another and, with Crean at the rear, slid down the steep slope. Incredibly, they made it virtually unscathed apart from a few scratches. It was the second time Crean had resorted to the dangers of sliding down ice slopes to save time, after the dramatic rescue of Teddy Evans on the *Terra Nova* expedition four years earlier. One has to wonder whether that episode played a part in encouraging his two companions to take a similar plunge this time.

Suffering still from the effects of their sixteen-day sea crossing from Elephant Island, progress was slow. But, when they heard the faint sound of a steam whistle that signalled the start of the working day at the whaling station, they realised they were nearing the end of their journey. After covering the shoreline of a frozen-over Fortuna Bay, the three men made their way on a snow-covered route heading towards Stromness. It was some time later that Crean's feet sank through the snow until he was up to his waist in frozen water - he had, in fact, descended into a lake, a lake that was later rechristened Crean Lake, in honour of the man who almost became victim to it.

Upon reaching the final ridge, they caught sight of Stromness whaling station and a whale-catcher steaming into the bay.

Their last hurdle was a waterfall and, using the rope, Tom Crean was the first to climb down, followed quickly by his two companions.

After a gruelling, energy-sapping, thirty-six hour trek, the heavily-bearded, raggedy, weather-beaten trio staggered into Stromness, where they encountered two young children, later revealed to be the daughters of the whaling station manager.[1] The children immediately turned and fled as if they'd just happened upon three zombies. Shortly after, they had a similar effect on a man to whom they tried beckoning. Finally, they encountered a Norwegian whaler who led them to the house of the whaling station manager. The man in charge, Thoralf Sorlle, who knew Shackleton having been acquainted with him before *Endurance* set sail from South Georgia back in December 1914, did not, at this moment, recognise the ragtag threesome stood at his door. One of the whalers, recounting the time he was present at this momentous scene, described the initial exchange of words:

"Sorlle asked: 'Who the hell are you?' and terrible bearded man in the centre of the three say very quietly: 'My name is Shackleton.' Me - I turn away and weep. I think manager weep too."[2]

After they imparted details of the incredible journey they had undertaken, he ushered them in and provided them comforts of which they had been deprived for what must have seemed like a lifetime.

Many of the whalers, who had gathered around to hear their story, shed tears as they imagined the terrible hardships to which the men had been subjected. After a hot bath, a change of clothes, haircuts, the luxury of a clean shave and a sumptuous meal, Crean and Shackleton retired to their beds, while Worsley accompanied a whaling boat crew to the other side of the island to pick up McNish, Vincent and McCarthy.

Time was now of the essence and, on 23rd May, Shackleton made the first of four attempts to reach his stranded crew on Elephant Island. Laid up for winter and moored at the island's Husvik whaling station was a large whaler, *Southern Sky*. After arranging clearance for its use and skippered by an old acquaintance of Shackleton's, Captain Ingvar Thom, Worsley, Crean, Shackleton and a number of whalers eager to volunteer their assistance boarded the vessel as she steamed out of the harbour. It soon became clear that the whaler was unable to penetrate the pack ice and, with coal provisions running low, the decision was made to abandon the attempt and head for the Falkland Islands.

On 31st May, *Southern Sky* arrived at Port Stanley where Shackleton met with the Governor who was keen to offer his full assistance.

Records document that Shackleton, Crean and Worsley boarded *HMS Avoca* on 1st June, a day after their return.[3] Diary entries of a steward serving on the vessel state that Shackleton's party visited for a meal and a change of clothes. Interestingly, the steward also reveals that the Royal Navy armed merchant cruiser was left on standby to make the next rescue attempt stating that they were *"expected to sail any minute to the rescue of Shackleton's men left stranded on Elephant Island."*[4]

It was an effort that never got underway for reasons we are left to speculate about.

Unfortunately, no other ship capable of undertaking an effective attempt at rescue was berthed at the island and Shackleton could do little but satisfy himself that the party at Elephant Island were able to survive on the rations they had which could be supplemented on a diet of the island's penguins.

It was while in the Falkland Islands that Shackleton first learned about the fate of the *Aurora*, the second expedition ship that had entered Cape Evans Bay on the Ross Sea side of Antarctica in January 1915. It made for disappointing reading as he discovered there was now another group of marooned men of the Ross Sea party, left exposed to the freezing elements and with an uncertain future.

At the new Town Hall on 3rd June 1916, one of the largest crowds Port Stanley had ever seen, congregated to hear Shackleton's account of the story so far. Beside him on the stage was Frank Worsley and Tom Crean, whose presence was highlighted in the *Falkland Island Magazine* with reference to his, by now, famous, life-saving march.[5]

At the end of his talk the magazine reported that Shackleton was: *"heartily cheered in recognition of the pluck exhibited by him and his intrepid companions."*

With two groups of men now stranded in the south's harsh, unforgiving environment, the weight of responsibility must have laid heavy on shoulders of the three men now desperate to arrange the rescue of their marooned colleagues.

After an offer had been received and accepted from the Uruguayan government to provide a trawler, *Instituto De Pesca No.1,* the second attempt got underway the day after her arrival in the Falklands on 16th June. Again, within twenty miles of reaching the island, the trawler had no means of penetrating the ice barrier that halted their progress. With just three day's supply of coal left, they barely made the journey back to the Falklands.

With the delays of rescue laying heavy on the minds of the three men and still no vessel available to them in the Falklands, they boarded the mailboat *Orita* and headed to Punta Arenas, Chile, where they hoped their fortunes would change.

As they sailed into the port on 4th July, the local news publication, The Magellan Times, reported their arrival, the description of which applied a little embellishment of Tom Crean's superhuman exploits:

> *"Sir Ernest Shackleton is accompanied by Captain F. A. Worsley and Mr Tom Crean. This is the third expedition of the latter, who received the Albert Medal from the King for saving the life of Captain Evans, whom he pulled for 200 miles over the ice."*

Within days, and with the financial assistance of the British community who'd raised £1,500, Shackleton chartered *Emma,* a wooden schooner with an auxiliary oil engine, and, in an effort to conserve on fuel, they set forth towed by a small steamer, *Yelcho,* under the kind offer of the Chilean Government. In poor weather, they set out on their mission of rescue on 12th July. In the heavy gales that ensued, the tow rope snapped and *Yelcho,* with her bilges waterlogged, was granted leave to return to the safety of port.

The *Emma,* now unaccompanied, sailed on. Tossing violently

in the storms that whipped up the waves around them, the motors seized up. The vessel was now entirely dependent on her sails and they continued south. Having reached close to 100 miles of Elephant Island and incapable of forcing a way through the pack ice, yet another futile attempt was abandoned.

Emma sailed back into Port Stanley on 8*th* August 1916.

It had been reported, on 20*th* July 1916, that *Discovery*, "*the only available vessel that could possibly reach Elephant Island party in time to save their lives,*" was being prepared for the rescue attempt. Under the command of Lieutenant James Fairweather, who came from a Dundee family of whalers, the ship and her commander were well-suited for the relief task ahead. *Discovery* departed England on 10*th* August and the plan was to pick up Shackleton, Crean and Worsley before heading on to Elephant Island. It was estimated she would reach the stranded men in October. The relief operation had a hidden objective and the publicity surrounding its mission was considered of great value to the Admiralty. Great care was taken to ensure the mission and the rescue would be filmed and photographed and, as *Discovery* left Plymouth Sound, the Admiralty issued orders for ships to cheer as she passed them.

Effectively, the staged rescue would have greatly affected the value of the expedition to Shackleton who was indebted to a number of financial contributors on his return.

Shackleton had only learned of the *Discovery* relief expedition on his return to Port Stanley aboard *Emma,* yet he knew it was a schedule, and a mission, that could have met with a very different ending on reaching the shores of Elephant Island. The survival of the stranded men was his sole concern and another plan for their quick rescue had to be the priority.

Under tow from the *Yelcho*, the schooner *Emma* arrived back in Punta Arenas on 14th August. Shackleton, increasingly aware of a potential tragedy occurring on Elephant Island, requested use of the *Yelcho* in a last-ditch attempt at rescue.

On 25th August, Shackleton, Crean and Worsley left Punta Arenas aboard the *Yelcho*.

With good fortune and fine weather in their favour, five days later, on 30th August, they finally found a path through the ice.

Looking out to the shore from the ship were Shackleton, Crean and Worsley. They were able to count the full crew who, over two years since leaving Plymouth, were frantically waving to them from the shore. One can only imagine the emotions at play as the group on shore witnessed Shackleton and Tom Crean sailing towards them in the lifeboats. It was 1 p.m. and, by 2 p.m., all the stranded shore party were aboard the ship heading north. The culmination of the greatest survival and rescue tale in maritime history was playing out its final act. Incredibly, not one man had been lost.

Consequently, the relief mission of *Discovery* proved in vain and, after reaching Montevideo in September, the skipper, Fairweather, learned of the rescue. She sailed back into Devonport on 29th November 1916 and was decommissioned.

As *Yelcho* steamed into the Chilean port of Punta Arenas on 3rd September 1916, a fanfare of some of the largest crowds ever witnessed in the town cheered loudly as brass bands played, marking the ship's approach. The people were there to see their heroes, every last one of them, including the captain of the *Yelcho*, pilot Luis Pardo, who, to this day, is feted and celebrated as a national hero in Chile.

Pardo was later offered a reward by the British Government, reputed to be £25,000, a huge amount for the time.[6] Yet, the reluctant hero declined it, stating, *"I was only doing my job."*

Central to this epic rescue tale were the names Shackleton, Worsley and Tom Crean, the Kerryman who had, on two previous occasions, been a primary player in saving the lives of expedition colleagues while serving in Antarctica. Cabling to the Daily Chronicle shortly after their arrival in the port, Shackleton wrote:

"With Wild lies the credit for having kept the party together in strength and safety under the most trying of conditions and I can not speak too highly of Crean and Worsley who had seen the thing through."[7]

Crean's reputation among his polar colleagues had now become firmly established but his story would not reach a public audience. Recognition was reserved for expedition leaders in an era when the class system determined who deserved glory. Despite numerous local newspaper accounts of Crean's heroic exploits in the following decades, it would be over 83 years before his name would come to the wider public's attention.

As a postscript to the tale of the perilous trek across South Georgia, Shackleton, Crean and Worsley all felt a *"fourth presence"* was guiding them to safety.

Shackleton's recollection was as follows:

"When I look back at those days, I have no doubt that providence guided us, not only across those snowfields but across the storm-white Sea that separated Elephant Island from our landing place on South Georgia. I know that, during that long and racking march of 36 hours over the unnamed mountains and glaciers of South Georgia, it seemed to me, often, that we

were four, not three. I said nothing to my companions on the point, but afterwards Worsley said to me, 'Boss, I had a curious feeling on the march that there was another person with us.' Crean confessed to the same belief. One feels the dearth of human words, the roughness of mortal speech in trying to describe things intangible but a record of our journeys would be incomplete without a reference to a subject very near to our hearts."[8]

Years later, long after he had left the navy, Tom Crean, on one of those rare occasions that he reminisced about his time in Antarctica, confided to his great friend, Bob Knightly, the Annascaul train station master, this same story. Crean, a man of strong faith who wore a holy scapular around his neck throughout his life, concluded, *"The Lord brought us home."*

With a number of his *Endurance* colleagues, Crean boarded the vessel, *Highland Laddie,* on a free-of-charge passage, courtesy of Nelson Line's Buenos Aires-based owners. On 8th November 1916, they arrived at Tilbury Docks, London.

Speaking to a Reuters correspondent on their return, Frank Wild gave a dramatic summary of their ordeal; beginning his story by telling the reporter of an incident where Orde-Lees' life was threatened by a huge twelve-foot leopard seal chasing him across ice floes. Taking a leaf out of Tom Crean's book, an ice-floe-hopping Wild caught them up and shot the seal before it managed to kill his colleague.

He told the correspondent:

"Elephant Island is the most inhospitable place on the face of the earth, although we were pretty glad to reach it when we did for many of the party were on the verge of collapse. From the physically fittest of them were chosen the five who accompanied

Sir Ernest in the open boat journey to South Georgia. The trip to South Georgia was, in my opinion, the finest thing ever done.

From the calculations made, I expected an attempt to rescue us towards the end of May but the ice conditions were so bad that there was no hope of it succeeding. Then I figured out he would try to get a wooden ship and return later. In my diary, I fixed August 25th as the approximate date. The actual date Sir Ernest took us off was the 30th. Of course, we had no idea that this was his fourth attempt.

We were just assembling for lunch to the call of 'Lunch O' and I was serving out the soup which was particularly good that day, consisting of boiled seal's backbone, limpets and seaweed, when there was another hail from Marston of 'Ship O.' Some of the men thought it was 'Lunch O' over again but when there was another yell from Marston, lunch had no further attraction."

He went on to state:

"The chief and Crean with some Chilean sailors were soon along-side in a boat. A pretty heavy sea was running but we didn't waste much time in getting aboard and in less than an hour we were steaming north."[9]

An account Wild gave at the offices of The Observer, after his return to England, provides a vivid description of the ordeal of the stranded men:

"We got to Elephant Island on April 9th and landed on the 15th on a narrow spit of shore a hundred and fifty yards long - the only place on that side of the island where we could have landed, for the cliffs rose perpendicularly 3,000 to 5,000 feet.

It seemed impossible to live on the spit of land, for the winds were so strong that we could not put up a suitable building and the low parts of the shore had previously been washed over by the sea. So, we began digging the ice hole, in which Sir Ernest, as you have read, left us.

For three weeks, the work kept us fairly busy. We dug about 15 or 16ft into a small glacis, or slope. We had got the place almost big enough to live in when we found there was water running - a sub-ice stream - and every blow we gave filled the entrance right up with snow. It would take us half a day each day to get the snow removed.

In the end, we found it quite impossible to make a habitation and we just had to chance being washed off the spit.

There, we made a hut by building two stone walls and laying the boats on them fore and aft and using the torn canvass of the tents in which we had been living for the roof and side.

We got this hut in weatherproof condition in something like a week. The roof, however, was no more than 4ft high and we suffered for a long time from stiff backs. Nor was the accommodation any too great. The floor space was only 18ft by 12ft for the whole party of 22. Five slept on the thwarts of one boat and six on the thwarts of the other. The rest on the floor - a floor of pebbles from the beach.

Though the party suffered a great deal from exposure before reaching the island, the only cases of illness were those due to frostbite for which eight members had to be treated. Hudson's fingers were very bad and Blackborrow had to have five toes amputated.

We lived principally on penguins and seals. Seals, however, were very scarce owing to an ice foot forming all round the shop and preventing them getting up and penguins in the soft snow were difficult to catch.

For five months at a time on the island, there was nothing to do. We had very few books and no games. But we had one banjo and, on Saturday nights, we always had some little sing-song and toasted wives and sweethearts. It is an old custom which we have always kept up on our expeditions.

The strongest drink for months was tea and, for a long time, we did not even have that, hot water and sugar being the substitute.

Sugar was served out three lumps to each man, four times a week and we used to save one of these allowances for the Saturday night toast."

Describing a typical day, Wild said:

"The cook turned out at seven o'clock and usually took until ten to get breakfast ready. This meal consisted nearly always of penguin steaks and penguin legs, the steaks being fried in blubber and the legs boiled in water. If it was a bad day, everyone remained in the sleeping bags except the cooks and lunch would be served to each man at one o'clock. Lunch four times a week was a biscuit and three pieces of sugar, two days a week it was nothing at all and, on the remaining day, it was nut food.

If the weather continued bad, all hands remained in sleeping bags and for dinner, another meat meal was served between five and six. By six o'clock, we were generally in bed. In the midwinter month, June-July, there was only four hours' daylight.

On fine days, the meals were served about the same time and, after breakfast, if there were any penguins or seals, the men would kill and skin them. In the afternoon, they went out for a walk which was always limited to about 100 yards as the spit terminated to a mound a hundred-foot high. The main part of the island was quite inaccessible.

Our lamp oil was made of blubber, the oil being poured into old sardine tins. Surgical bandages that had been used for the cases of frostbite, supplied the wick. The lamps made a red flame and an awful smoke, offering no inducement to sit up late.

In all the months of waiting we never once lost hope of relief, The confidence of the whole party in Sir Ernest Shackleton and his luck was tremendous and, one morning, at the end of August, when we had only three days meat in hand and very little else, we saw a ship passing and knew that our faith was justified."[10]

For Shackleton, however, the task of rescue was not over, and he made his way to New Zealand. Oblivious to the futility of their depot-laying mission from the opposite side of the continent, the Ross Sea supporting party of ten men had, themselves, become stranded, as their ship, *Aurora*, had become stuck fast in the ice near Cape Evans, Captain Scott's former base.

After arriving at Cape Crozier on 9th January 1915, *Aurora* suffered a torrid time navigating through pack ice among heavy swells and currents as she dropped offshore parties for their mission to lay the depots for Shackleton's crossing team.

Battered by continuous Antarctic storms, the ship later became gripped by the ice and, with her engines out of commission, on 6th May, in a hurricane force blizzard, a tidal crack onshore broke the ship from her moorings close to Cape Evans.

She drifted out helplessly into the Southern Ocean and all attempts to alert the shore party by wireless failed. By July 1915, *Aurora* was caught between floes 8ft thick as she continued northward imprisoned by the ice. In command of the ship, Lieutenant Joseph Stenhouse and his crew tried to ease the pressure to prevent the vessel from being crushed. At one point they resorted to pouring sulphuric acid on the surrounding ice but it was an effort made in vain.

With prospects looking dire, *Aurora* seemed destined for a similar fate to the *Endurance* which would later be doomed to an icy grave on the opposite side of the continent.

The ship's crew were equipped for the immediate abandonment and Stenhouse reported that: *"Our chances of emerging safely seemed small."*

Perilously close to the end, when a force of thirty large bergs were closing in on the ship, she finally broke free from the ice on 14th March 1916 and headed for New Zealand. After another hazardous journey, she limped back, under tow, into Port Chalmers on 3rd April where she underwent a costly refit.

Despite the loss of their ship, the stranded party valiantly continued their depot-laying tasks unaware of the fate of *Endurance*. *Aurora* was to have been their living quarters and she still carried most of the provisions and equipment for their mission. They had little choice but to improvise; they utilised clothing and equipment in the hut, left over from previous expeditions, that had been both Scott's and Shackleton's base.

Sticking to their task and unaware of the cessation of the mission of the *Endurance* party, they continued but their harrowing efforts in worsening conditions came at the loss of three men: the leader, Mackintosh, along with Hayward and Spencer-Smith.

The ordeal for the marooned Ross Sea party ended on 10th January 1917, when the refitted and repaired *Aurora*, with Shackleton aboard, returned to rescue the remaining seven members. It was only then that they discovered the drama that had been played out on the opposite side of the continent.

On their return to London in the middle of a World War, Elephant Island survivor, George Marston, who Shackleton had recruited as the artist for the expedition, conveyed the shock of events that had occurred during their absence from civilisation in a touching narrative:

From Nowhere to London

"At last we are steaming up the Thames - not, as we had dreamed of doing, in our own vessel, bringing back the fruits of two years' endeavour, but in a huge iron ship crammed with frozen meat, a minute contribution to the appetite of a nation. We sail in a world of darkness and silence, past spots where we know busy towns exist. We are challenged, examined and passed by pugnacious, self-confident small craft. We enter docks in silence and darkness and, overhead, the beams of searchlights make ever-changing patterns of light.

Two years ago, we had left home to follow the white trail of the frozen South, to add our tiny efforts to the work which began with life on earth and is still unfinished. We left London when the declaration of war by England was imminent. On leaving our last port of call in South Georgia, we heard of Belgium's fall, of the invaders' sweep on Paris and of their final check. The Battle of the Marne had been fought. And, there, for us, the curtain fell.

The white lands of the South claimed us but nature brought our plans to nought. With our ship crushed, our gear scattered, we eventually reached land in our boats with a minute supply of food, there to lie in wet discomfort for four-and-a-half months. Getting into touch once more with the outer world, our senses were stunned by the amazing facts we were called upon to accept. To us, the world seemed mad and we its only sane members. While news of the daily happenings of the war were being carried to all corners of the earth by every means known to science or by the efforts of the humble runners of the outposts of civilisation, we were perhaps the only human beings who were in total ignorance of the happenings of those two years. We had lived the life of primitive man battling with nature for existence. Politics and innumerable small worries of civilisation were, for us, a thing of the past. The fact that nations were fighting for their very existence was a mere shadowy thought. Our struggle with nature had readjusted our minds to the narrow outlook of our forefathers. While civilisation had been led step by step to accept, as natural everyday occurrences, the events of the most bitter war in the world's history, our speculations had narrowed.

The familiar appearance of our advertisement pages, with their everlasting trivialities, suggest, at first, that nothing had occurred to break the placid smallness of everyday life. From the gloomy tale of the pessimist to the jaunty tale of the fatuous optimist; from the terrible array of facts and figures to the irrepressible humour from the very trenches themselves - all appeared inconsistent and bewildering. And, during our unavoidably slow return, many were the eager inquiries we made of chance acquaintances from home and many were the conflicting reports we received. Perhaps not until entering the London docks in silence and darkness - fascinated by the searchlights as they swept across the sky, peering behind every little cloud for lurking danger - did we realise that war was a reality, that the very clouds themselves must now be regarded as a possible menace.

The depth of the change in the life of London dawned on us gradually. Day by day, small unfamiliar incidents multiplied until we felt strangers in our own homes. By day, the streets present more or less their old aspect but the stream of traffic is thinned and the discarded hansoms and four-wheelers have come back. Women have got the chance to show what they can do and, nobly, they have responded. We are filled with admiration for their obvious capability. The armed guards on our railways and docks; the warnings to the public in railways carriages; the convalescent soldiers in the street; the searchlights which scan the sky and the cheerful way in which dark, clear nights are spoken of as "Good Zep weather", all combine to overpower the home-comer with strangeness. The cheerful willingness of the people to bear greater and greater burdens, to sacrifice, one after another, treasured privileges is wonderful when viewed from our perspective.

The stress of the past two years is, we feel, responsible for the air of increased consideration everywhere in evidence. People seem now to have a bond of friendship arising from a common cause."

George Marston[11]

On his return from his polar exploits, Shackleton was commissioned by the British government in the capacity of a special, temporarily assigned rank of Major. Because of his expertise in cold climes, in late 1918, he was assigned a role as part of the North Russia Expedition force, the mission of which was to halt the advance of the Bolsheviks. His duties, in the Arctic conditions, were to supervise clothing and to train the military in measures that maintained their good health.

Returning to England in March 1919 and adding to his long list of international honours, he was appointed an Officer of the Order of the British Empire (OBE) in May. In October 1919, he was discharged from the army, retaining the rank of Major.

Commencing in late 1919, Shackleton embarked upon a lecture tour, making use of Hurley's pioneering footage shot while on the *Endurance* expedition. On Boxing Day 1919, he gave the first of a series of twice-daily, two-hour performances for six days a week at the Royal Philharmonic Hall, London, entertaining audiences with tales of his experiences.[12] It was an exhausting schedule that continued for five months and the proceeds helped pay for the liabilities of the failed expedition.

In February 1920, for the one hundredth performance, nine of his former expedition colleagues took to the stage with him. Among them were Frank Wild, Frank Worsley and Tom Crean.[13]

CHAPTER 5

Shackleton's Birth -
In a letter sent to the
editor of the Daily News
shortly after news broke
of Shackleton's death.

'Sir, the only time I
heard Shackleton speak
was in London, in April
1920, and, after his
lecture, he asked for
questions as usual.
One was: *"What is your
nationality?"* and
his answer, as nearly as
I can remember, was:
*"What country do I
belong to? I belong to
that distressful country,
Ireland. Poor Ireland!"*

*Irish Examiner, 11th
February, 1922*

When life on the lecture circuit ended, the obsessive adventurer turned his thoughts to a return to exploration and his sights, this time, were to head north to the Arctic.

Frank Worsley joined the war effort after the expedition and served out a distinguished career throughout the First and Second World Wars. Like Shackleton and Crean, he served on the North Russia Expeditionary force, and he met up with both men during his time there. In August of 1919, his navigational skills saw him lead a group of twenty-five men to safety when they became lost in a forest with two hundred Bolsheviks hot on their trail. Among his many awards, he received an OBE. The Poles indeed proved magnetic for men like Shackleton, Crean and Worsley, the latter of whom returned in 1925, this time as skipper of the British Arctic Expedition aboard the expedition ship *Island*.

After a life that saw him undertake lecture tours, write a number of successful books about his experiences and partake in a mission to seek lost treasure on the Cocos Islands, Frank Worsley died in Claygate, Surrey, on 1st February 1943.

Harry McNish, Timothy McCarthy and John Vincent made their return from South Georgia and reached London on 3rd August

1916. All three men were fulsome in their praise of Shackleton and remained confident that the stranded men on Elephant Island, under the leadership of Frank Wild, would hold out until relief arrived.[14]

After a short period of leave, Tim McCarthy was called up to the Royal Navy Reserve as an Able Seaman. On 16th March 1917, while serving as a gunner aboard the tanker *SS Narragansett,* he was one of forty-six men killed after the tanker was torpedoed by a German U-Boat off the south coast of Ireland.

The man Shackleton described as *"the best and most efficient of the sailors, who was always cheerful under the most trying of circumstances"*, was just 29 years old. Today, a memorial bust in his hometown of Kinsale commemorates his and his brother, Mortimer's, achievements while serving on Antarctic expeditions in the company of their countryman, Tom Crean.

After his return, Birmingham-born John Vincent joined the Royal Naval Reserve in 1917. A trawler man before joining the crew of *Endurance,* between the wars, Vincent returned to skippering boats out of his adopted city of Grimsby. He, again, signed on with the Royal Navy Reserve in 1940 where he took charge of an armed trawler, *HM Trawler Alfredian*. While aboard, he caught pneumonia and was transported to Grimsby's naval hospital. He died on 19th January 1941.

Harry 'Chippy' McNish, the ship's carpenter, rejoined the Merchant Navy after the expedition and he later left England to work in New Zealand. Working for a shipping company, he regularly complained of aching bones, which he put down to his ordeal in the Antarctic. Eventually, he was forced to give up work, due to an injury and his life went on a downward spiral. He lived out the remainder of his life in poverty, assisted by monthly contributions from the dockworkers of Wellington.

Baden Norris, founder of Lyttelton Museum, New Zealand, recalled when, as a youngster accompanying his father, he was taken to the bedside of a dying McNish:

"I recall this small, dark room... McNish gestured to us... come to his bedside. I was terrified. My father held my hand. He wanted to honour McNish, the hardworking carpenter who had survived Antarctica's most dramatic shipwreck. McNish wanted to tell us something. He could barely raise his head from the pillow and leaned his face close to mine. In a hoarse whisper, he said, 'Shackleton killed my cat.'

It was a sad ending for the man who, along with John Vincent and two other crew members of the expedition, was denied a Polar Medal. Although it appeared a harsh decision by

Miraculous Escape

SIR E SHACKLETON'S REMARK-ABLE RE-APPEARANCE.

News of the re-appearance of Sir Earnest Shackleton was received about midnight on Thursday, and came as a dramatic surprise.

It was first communicated to the King, and then to Lady Shackleton, who was overjoyed at the news of her husband's safety. Long since all hope had been abandoned of the return of the " Endurance," and grave apprehensions were felt about the safety of the explorers.

Messages to hand to-day show that the expedition had had a miraculous escape.

After meeting almost unprecedented weather in the early part of 1915, the " Endurance" was badly nipped by great bergs, and afterwards foundered. Sir E Shackleton succeeded in getting off all his men and some stores.

Terrible privations were suffered, and after a journey of great hazard the explorers reached Elephant Island, one of the westernmost islands of the South Shetland group, at about 50 miles from Falkland Islands, the nearest point of civilisation.

There was great scarcity of food, and Shackleton then decided to leave the greater part of his men with rations in an icehole, which was dug on the island, while he set off for help in a small boat with five companions. After a journey of three weeks of extraordinary peril, he reached South Georgia. Here he sought aid of the whalers to rescue his companions on Elephant Island.

This was impossible owing to the weather conditions prevailing. Urgent help is needed for the marooned men. Sir Ernest has not lost one of his expedition.

Kerry Sentinel 3rd June 1916

Shackleton, who demanded loyalty from those serving under him, rewarding a man who had fleetingly rebelled against his leader could, in his estimation, have set a potentially dangerous precedent. Undoubtedly, the skills of McNish in adapting the *James Caird* to undertake the sea crossing to South Georgia were vital. Missing out on a Polar Medal was perhaps down to his earlier insubordination and was most likely triggered by Shackleton's order to kill the ship's cat. With the passing of time, a decision to award McNish the medal posthumously would, I believe, be a fair one.

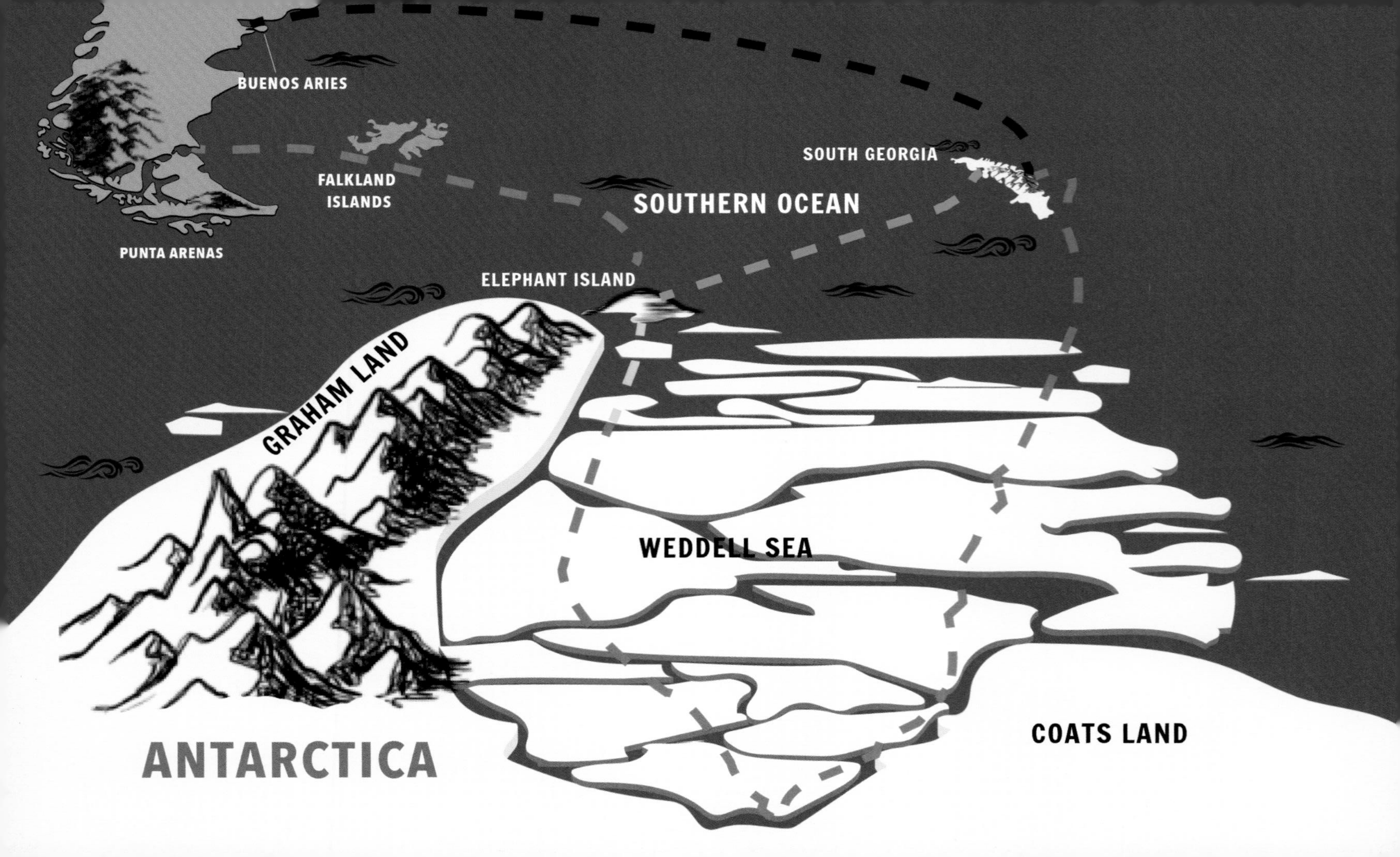
BUENOS ARIES
FALKLAND ISLANDS
PUNTA ARENAS
SOUTH GEORGIA
SOUTHERN OCEAN
ELEPHANT ISLAND
GRAHAM LAND
WEDDELL SEA
COATS LAND
ANTARCTICA

TOM CREAN'S JOURNEY WITH SHACKLETON 1914-1916

26TH OCTOBER 1914
ENDURANCE SAILS FROM BUENOS AIRES TO SOUTH GEORGIA

21ST NOVEMBER 1915
FROM SOUTH GEORGIA TO THE WEDDELL SEA - ENDURANCE BECOMES ICEBOUND, DRIFTS NORTH AND SINKS

9TH APRIL 1916
THREE LIFEBOATS, THE DUDLEY DOCKER, STANCOMB WILLS AND JAMES CAIRD ARE ROWED TO ELEPHANT ISLAND

24 APRIL 1916
A SIX-MAN CREW, INCLUDING TOM CREAN, SAIL THE JAMES CAIRD LIFEBOAT 750 MILES TO SOUTH GEORGIA

19TH MAY 1916
TOM CREAN, ERNEST SHACKLETON AND FRANK WORSLEY TRAVERSE THE MOUNTAINS OF SOUTH GEORGIA

30TH AUGUST 1916
THE YELCHO PICKS UP THE 22 STRANDED MEN ON ELEPHANT ISLAND AND TAKES THEM TO PUNTA ARENAS

SHACKLETON'S MEN IN LONDON.

THE TERRIBLE VOYAGE FROM ELEPHANT ISLAND.

Reuter states that three members of the Shackleton Expedition reached London yesterday from South Georgia. They are Harry McNish, carpenter of the Endurance, and two seamen, Vincent and McCarthy. They were three of a volunteer crew of five who accompanied Sir Ernest Shackleton on his journey by whaleboat from Elephant Island on April 24, and eventually reached South Georgia. They are full of enthusiasm for Sir Ernest Shackleton. They say that but for his leadership not one would have survived. They speak with equal confidence of Frank Wild, who was left in charge of the marooned men on Elephant Island, and they express the belief that the men there will be able to hold out until relief arrives.

Before they reached Elephant Island Sir Ernest Shackleton had planned that it would be necessary to go to South Georgia. The journey from Elephant Island to South Georgia, which lasted fifteen days, is described as a terrible experience. Constantly they had to hack the ice from the boat to prevent her being engulfed. They had sufficient rations, but were very short of water. It was expected that they would meet icebergs, but not a single one was sighted.

The voyage was one of daily and hourly peril, but Sir Ernest Shackleton's proverbial luck seemed to prevent what looked like inevitable disaster. There were constant hurricanes and bad weather, and even as they set out from Elephant Island the whaleboat and its occupants were capsized. During the four days spent on Elephant Island McNish improvised a sort of shelter on the boat, and under this the men crept at intervals to snatch a little sleep. The men had their first square meal on South Georgia, where they secured some albatross.

The Guardian
4th August 1916

THE SHACKLETON EXPEDITION.

ANOTHER VOYAGE OF RESCUE.

Reuter's Agency states that a message has been received from Sir Ernest Shackleton from Chile stating that he is hastening the settlement of matters in connection with the Weddell Sea party of his expedition, so as to get over to Australia at the earliest possible moment. With the exception of the seaman who had his toes amputated, all the men taken off Elephant Island have recovered from their privations.

Through the generosity of the Commonwealth and New Zealand Governments, the Aurora, which it will be remembered broke away from the Ross barrier and drifted in the Antarctic pack for about ten months, is being repaired and refitted to go south to rescue the ten men of Captain Mackintosh's party marooned there.

The conditions of the ice in the Ross Sea vary from year to year, but it is thought that it will be inadvisable for the Aurora to start on her voyage to the south until at the earliest the middle of December.

Sir Ernest Shackleton feels the keenest personal responsibility for the ten men who were left on Ross Island when the Aurora broke loose. In one of his earliest letters from the Falkland Islands he announced that, in face of the disasters which had overtaken both sections of the expedition, he would not rest content until he had done everything humanly possible to save all the marooned men.

The Observer
17th September
1916

"

*Life without experience
and sufferings is not life*

"

Socrates

Chapter 6

TOM

POST-ANTARTICA

Shortly after his return from *Endurance,* Crean was specially promoted to Acting Boatswain on 27th December 1916 for services on the Antarctic Expedition. Naval records confirm that, after the New Year, he was aboard the flagship of the North Atlantic cruiser fleet, *HMS King Alfred,* and left the ship at Sierra Leone on the 14th February 1917.[1]

On this date, Crean's record states that he was ledgered to the shore-based *HMS Pembroke* at Chatham but his services were clearly needed elsewhere. Why his time aboard *King Alfred* is not documented remains a mystery but the busy port of Freetown was an important naval outpost in the battle for sea supremacy during the war, and it's possible that Crean's services as boatswain were employed on vessels protecting merchant ships which were being targeted by German U-Boats as they attempted to cross the Atlantic.

Shortly after his disembarkation at Sierra Leone, he returned to Ireland and, on 5th September 1917, at the age of 40, Tom Crean married Ellen Herlihy, a local girl he had known since childhood. They swapped wedding vows at the Sacred Heart Church in Annascaul.

MARRIAGE.

CREAN—HERLIHY—On 5th September, 1917, at the Church of the Sacred Heart, Annascaul, by the Rev. Denis O'Connor, P.P., Thomas Crean, son of Mr. and Mrs. P. Crean, Gortacurrane, to Ellie, sixth daughter of Mrs. and the late Mr. P. Herlihy, Annascaul.

Liberator 17th September 1917

Much of his naval career after marriage was spent in Ireland ledgered to the main depot ship *HMS Colleen*, where Crean was assigned to the sub-base at Berehaven, (now Castletownbere). It was a time and place that Crean appeared to have made many friends. In letters to Ralph Dodds, an army Captain, who was also stationed there, Crean reminisced about his time in Antarctica. Dodds, who, himself, had earned awards for bravery after being wounded at the front in France in 1915, was fascinated by the southern expeditions and his friend could offer him an account of them that no other man could. The letters also provide us with a rare opportunity to read Crean's own account on the demise of Scott's party on their return from the South Pole. In one correspondence from Crean, he reveals his plans to venture forth once more to Antarctica. In it, he writes: *"I have now fulfilled three expeditions and look forward to a fourth."*[2]

Dated September 3rd 1918 and in the first of two surviving letters written to Dodds, Crean wrote:

"Thanks very much indeed for the letter you sent to Guinness. It's very nicely put together and I hope you will have a good reply. In any case, you have made your point for me and I am very much obliged. With regards to Captain Scott, he reached the South Pole and the brave gentleman died on the 29th March, 1912. As I remember poor Captain Oates, it brings back old times to me. I will never forget him, the poor gentleman he lived and a hero he died. He died on the 16th or 17th March 1912 when he walked out of his tent into a blizzard, so as not to delay his comrades. And, when Captain Scott asked him where he was going, he answered him 'I am only going out for a minute sir.'

Yours respectfully, Tom Crean"

The letter Dodds had sent to Guinness was, no doubt, in relation to the licensed premises Crean had recently bought in Annascaul and, whatever the outcome of his enquiry, 84 years later, the company saw fit to utilise Crean's story in the promotion of their famous drink. To obtain permission for the use of Crean's name and story, it was, ironically, Guinness, on this occasion, who were sending the letters to his descendants.

In their short time together as expedition colleagues, Crean had enjoyed a good relationship with Lawrence Oates, known as 'Titus', a nickname given him by his *Terra Nova* shipmates.

Together, they shared a love of animals and they may have reminisced about a time when Oates had reportedly once ridden at Tralee's Ballyvelly racecourse close to Crean's home.[3]

Tom also used his time out on shore-leave to visit a navy colleague, Dave Moriarty, who lived at The Square in the town. They knew one another from old after serving together at the Devonport navy barracks, *HMS Vivid*, and they spent many hours chatting and catching up with one another.[4]

Dave's son, Daniel, who later joined the priesthood and rose to become a Canon of the Catholic diocese in Surrey, recalled how Crean, a frequent visitor to his childhood home, had to wear heavy socks instead of shoes on account of the frostbite he had suffered from his time in Antarctica. It's likely that Crean's feet, at this stage, so soon after his return from Antarctica, were particularly painful and that the socks Dan refers to acted as a forerunner to the specially made boots he later wore. Dan also revealed that Tom was extremely popular with youngsters in the town who addressed him as 'Uncle Tom.' Crean's sojourn at Bere Island, as with any part of the world he made his home, was a time during which he left a huge impression on everyone who met him, regardless of their age.[5]

As early as 13th April 1917, Tom Crean, on shore-leave from the navy and Bere Island, had applied to the Dingle Quarter Session for the transfer of a liquor licence[6] and, later, with the help of his navy pension, he operated a licensed premises in his home village of Annascaul. Crean purchased the land and its buildings in 1916 from a local acquaintance, James Webb, whose father, a widower, had been residing alone in the property up till his death in 1912. Records later refer to it being named *Bridge House* but today it's more familiarly known as the *South Pole Inn*.

The day in the Dingle courthouse was also an opportunity for the very first Tom Crean fan to reveal himself, as the sitting Judge proclaimed, *"I am proud this man is a Kerryman. They've had some good men in Kerry, but this is an exceptional one."*

Granting the licence, the Judge went on to state, *"I am more than delighted and honoured to know such a man and I hope that we have such men in the county in the future as we have had in the past.*"[7]

> **Notice of Application to Quarter Sessions for a Certificate of Publican's Licence.**
>
> **TAKE NOTICE**, that it is my intention to apply at the next General Quarter Sessions of the Peace to be held at Dingle, in and for the Division of Tralee and County of Kerry, on the 13th day of April, 1917, for a Certificate to enable me to receive a Transfer of a Seven Day or Ordinary Licence to Sell Beer, Cider and Spirits by Retail, to be consumed on the Premises, at my Dwelling-house, situate at Anniscaul, Townland of Ardrinane, in the Parish of Ballinacourty, Barony of Corkaguiny and County of Kerry.
> Dated this 7th day of March, 1917.
>   THOMAS CREAN, Applicant.
>   JOHN KENNEDY, Solicitor for Applicant,
>   Dingle.

Liberator 17th March 1917

During his service in Ireland, he was confirmed in the role of Boatswain on 2nd January 1918. While ledgered to *HMS Colleen*, Tom Crean joined the crew of *HMS Inflexible* on 14th November 1918.[8] It was three days after the end of the First World War and Crean, in charge of quarterdeck duties, was onboard the battlecruiser as the German High Seas Fleet surrendered their ships at Scapa Flow on 21st November 1918.[9] On his release papers from Berehaven base on the 5th December 1918, he had been recommended for promotion by Commodore Hugh Heard, who described

Crean as *"A very zealous and capable officer and seaman."*[10]

For Crean, already confirmed as Warrant Officer on January 2nd 1918, further promotion to the commissioned ranks could still be made possible thanks to Admiral Fisher's earlier reforms that now provided men from the lower decks an opportunity to progress into the commissioned ranks.

Events in Ireland after the turn of the New Year saw the formation of a breakaway government and the first *Dáil Éireann* declared independence from Britain. The announcement, on 21st January 1919 would trigger the beginning of the Irish War of Independence, also referred to as The Tan War (*Cogadh na Saoirse*). It was a conflict that would rage on for almost two and a half years.

Tom Crean's penultimate naval appointment commenced on 14th March 1919, when he was assigned to *HMS Fox*. The ship was en route to Northern Russia as part of an expeditionary force to help prevent the rapid advance of the Bolsheviks.

In an area of strategic importance to the allies after the close of the First World War, troops fighting against the advance along the Dvina River, inland from the port of Archangel, required urgent relief and assistance. The mission of the navy flotilla under the command of Edward Altham, who also happened to be Crean's captain aboard *HMS Fox*, was to support the army and evacuate battle-weary troops.

It happened to be a time when the skills of Antarctic veteran Tom Crean would be called upon in the Arctic regions and we are left to wonder whether he was specifically singled out for the mission because of his vast experience in cold climates.

Certainly, with Shackleton's expertise having been commissioned by the British government in charge of clothing and equipment for the Northern Russia campaign and with a number of Crean's former *Endurance* colleagues, including Frank Worsley, also serving on the campaign, the evidence suggests so.

HMS Fox left Sheerness on 27th April 1919 and reached Rosyth on 29th April. After a five-day stay in which men were discharged to other ships and others transported to hospital, she headed out of harbour reaching Murmansk on 9th May, where she weighed anchor overnight.

On 10th May 1919, *HMS Fox* headed for Archangel where the heart of the fight against the Bolsheviks was being fought out but, within a day, she encountered a problem Crean had been all too familiar with in his career - she became icebound and fears for her survival grew as she creaked and groaned under the pressure.

Two accompanying ships in the flotilla were stuck fast and it must have brought back bad memories for Crean. However, rescue appeared the following day in the shape of two icebreakers that had been requested from Archangel to assist a third whose efforts to break up the twelve-feet-thick ice barrier had been largely ineffectual. Correspondence from the ship soon after this incident shows the crew were all aware of the officer aboard who had served with Scott and Shackleton and his high reputation had preceded him.[11]

Fox finally reached Archangel on 16th May 1919 and its time stuck in the ice allowed 'Mr Crean, sir', as he was now being addressed by those under his command, to pass on his expertise of the conditions.[12]

It was soon after that Tom Crean and Frank Worsley were reunited aboard *HMS Fox*. Worsley joined the ship on 8th June 1919 from *HMS Cricket* and, for almost a month, the two polar heroes served together once again, this time on an entirely different mission and in the northern hemisphere.[13] No doubt they were able to enthral the crew with a tale of rescue they had never before heard the like of.

Crean's duties saw him leave the ship on two occasions, leading a party of men up the northern Dvina River and his role was, more than likely, to resupply the forces attempting to hold back the Bolsheviks.[14]

The campaign in Northern Russia was brought to an end after a public and media outcry at the costs, both in money and in lives, over five hundred of which were lost. For Tom Crean, his time in Russia, albeit while serving in a supporting role, was his second experience in a field of conflict while in the employ of the Royal Navy.

On 27th September 1919, the flotilla headed home, having fulfilled its duties and evacuated allied forces in the area.[15]

Crean took up his final navy posting on 21st November 1919 aboard *HMS Hecla*, the depot ship and special torpedo vessel based at Portsmouth.

On 24th February, he was admitted to Chatham hospital with defective vision, having been diagnosed with retinitis.[16] His departure from the navy one month later, on 24th March 1920, was an enforced one and he was retired 'medically unfit.'[17] He had served almost twenty-seven of his forty-three years in the Royal Navy.

The day after Crean's retirement, the potential dangers ex-servicemen might face in their homeland in the midst of the Tan War was highlighted when his former *Terra Nova* colleague, Robert Forde, became the victim of a shooting. Luckily for Forde, who was on a visit to Limerick a month after his own retirement, the bullet pierced only his clothing and he sustained no injuries.[18]

The perpetrators of the attack, three youths who fled the scene immediately after the shot was fired, were never identified and the reasons for the shooting remain unknown.

Forde had been greatly missed by his *Terra Nova* colleagues after an enforced return from Antarctica eight years earlier, in April 1912, necessitated by severe frostbite in his hand. Forde made a recovery, yet the extent of his injury forced him to wear a protective glove for the remainder of his life. Scott valued his contributions highly and, in his absence, stated that no one could replace him. He eventually returned to naval duty where he was promoted to Chief Petty Officer and he died in his hometown of Cobh in 1959.

The latter part of 1920 would most likely have been the period that Crean's polar services were once again sought, as Sir Ernest came calling.

As early as January 1921, Shackleton announced plans for his next expedition. Initially, he contemplated going to the Arctic but, by the end of June, his plans had changed and south, once more, was to be his final destination.

For the purpose, he had purchased a Norwegian two-masted sloop called *Foca 1* and had renamed it *Quest*. To generate public interest, it was reported that part of the mission would be to try and locate a lost island, Tuanaki, from which, according to legend, the Maoris of New Zealand had originated. Drumming up publicity for his adventures and expeditions was a specialist trait of Shackleton, the master promoter, and the quest to discover a mystery island would no doubt have found its way into his repertoire of anecdotes that helped fill the halls and theatres in which he appeared.

As before, he requested Crean to be at his side for the expedition but, this time, Tom declined, telling Shackleton, "*I have a long-haired pal now.*"

It must have been a disappointment for Shackleton, who had already allocated his fellow Irishman a role in charge of the boats and it's clear that Crean's earlier ambitions to serve on a fourth expedition had, by this time, changed. He had settled back into family life and resisted any temptations he may have had to join Shackleton.

It happened also to coincide with turbulent times in Ireland and this must have played a major part in Crean's decision. The Tan War was still raging and, with young daughters to care for, Crean made the decision any protective father would.

On 13th April 1920, Tom Crean was present among huge crowds staging a two-day protest in the town of Tralee, County Kerry, against the maltreatment of almost 100 Irish Republican prisoners in Dublin's Mountjoy jail.[19] A week earlier, on 5th April, the men had gone on hunger strike and a concerted effort to provide support for their plight had led to an organised general strike across Ireland. Mindful of the death of Thomas Ashe, who had himself refused food to his last breath just two-and-a-half years before, over 40,000 turned out in support of their incarcerated countrymen. It was reported that many of the demonstrators amassing around the prison were women clutching at rosary beads while praying for the well-being of the hunger strikers.

Tralee, like other towns and cities, called a lightning strike bringing about cessation of all trade and labour; no trains ran, no shops or bars opened.

The large gathering in the town witnessed the first time former sailors and soldiers protested publicly alongside their compatriots in support of fellow Irishmen.

The crowds braved a deluge of downpours over the course of the two days and the protest passed without incident. On the second day, the huge gathering learnt that they had won the release of the prisoners and the 5,000 people who had converged on the town celebrated.

The article confirming Crean's attendance stated:

> *"Among visitors stranded in Tralee, owing to the absence of railway facilities, was Mr Crean of Annascaul. a famous man who was with the Shackleton Expedition to the South Pole."*

This could be interpreted as though Crean had been caught up in the middle of the protest accidentally but I believe the truth to be very different. His best friend, Robert Knightly, was the stationmaster at Annascaul who, the day before, had been fully versed that the trains would not be running. Crean, before boarding the train to Tralee (like everyone else at the gathering) would have had prior knowledge that the protest would be taking place. It is my strong opinion that making the journey to Tralee on a day when the weather was that of a continual two-day downpour was not for the purpose of browsing the shops.

Crean's presence at the protest gives us another glimpse of his character and his loyalties. Although he was not the only ex-sailor or soldier there on the day, he was, no doubt, among the most notable, and one has to presume that he did not care whether he was reproached by either the authorities for attending or by his peers for having once served in the Royal Navy. Whatever his mindset on the morning as he made the twenty-mile journey to Tralee, he was clearly intent on adding his voice to object to the treatment of his countrymen.

It remains an indication of how passionate he was about Ireland and how committed he was to fair play and justice.

One can only guess the conflicting feelings he might have felt twelve days later, on 25th April, when his brother Cornelius, a Sergeant in the Royal Irish Constabulary, was shot dead during an IRA ambush in Upton, County Cork. It later transpired that Cornelius'

wife, Annie Stanton Crean, had urged him to resign on the night before his murder. She had become alarmed at recent occurrences and
was concerned for the safety of her husband.[20]

It had been barely one month after Tom had retired, and the
loss of his older brother must have been a devastating blow to Crean,
who attended the funeral three days later with his brother, Daniel,
and his youngest sister, Catherine.[21]

Cornelius had become another victim of the Irish War of Independence, which had seen the introduction of the Black and Tans,
a despised group of British Army veterans of the First World War,
who were employed by the British government to reinforce RIC forces
during the conflict.

The brutality of the Black and Tans still today evokes bitter
memories at the mere mention of their name. Their deployment of
heinous tactics served only to unite the vast majority of Irishmen and
women on the path for freedom from Crown governance.

It was also around this time that the Crean home became the tar-
get of a Black and Tans visit. It is possible that the visit was prompted
by Crean's presence at the 12th April Tralee protest in support of the
hunger strikers, although there is no firm evidence of the date the raid
took place.

With their suspicions aroused, the Black and Tans ransacked the
home and it was only when they happened upon evidence of Crean's
time in the Royal Navy that they called a halt to the raid.

Continuing the catalogue of events that would document 1920
as being as stormy as any of the years he'd spent in Antarctica, in late
September, Tom Crean was called as a witness in the courtroom at
Victoria Barracks in County Cork. Crean, along with a host of other
witnesses, testified in the case of two Annascaul men accused of an

attack on a British Army patrol in August 1920. In a case that served to highlight the divisiveness of the conflict, one of the accused, who had two brothers serving in the RIC, refused to recognise the court. He was subsequently sentenced to three years' penal servitude. The other man, a neighbour of Crean's, was released as a result of the testimonies of the witnesses.[22]

While Crean's retirement did not have the peaceful start he would have planned, the turn of the New Year provided him with cause for celebration as his niece, Mary Crean, daughter of his late brother Hugh, was married at the Sacred Heart Church in Annascaul on 22nd January 1921.

His friend, Shackleton, had headed south again leaving St Katherine's Dock in London on 17th September 1921. Less than four months after setting sail and a day after reaching Grytviken harbour in South Georgia, the great explorer drew his last breath.

Sir Ernest Shackleton died in his cabin after suffering a fatal heart attack on 5th January 1922, during his final expedition south aboard *Quest*. His coffin was transferred to the steamer, *Professor Gruvel*, on 17th January and taken to Montevideo, Uruguay, in preparation for a departure to England on 11th February.[23]

He had been laid in a simple coffin constructed from deal (fir or pinewood) and lined with corrugated zinc. It was made by the whalers of South Georgia for the hero they knew as 'Canny Jack', due to his reluctance to take any unnecessary risks. A squad of Uruguayan soldiers remained by the coffin as a guard of honour for the explorer who had generated an army of admirers throughout his remarkable life of adventure.[24]

Leonard, now Captain Hussey, a crew member who served under Shackleton on both *Endurance* and *Quest*, accompanied the body to Uruguay. While there, he received news that Lady Shackleton wished, as her husband had expressed to her many times, for his body to be buried at Grytviken Cemetery. The coffin was transferred to the barque, *Woodville*, on 15th February and was returned to South Georgia. Sir Ernest Shackleton was buried in the Norwegian cemetery there on 5th March 1922.[25]

The news must have saddened Crean deeply; yet, there's no written account of his reaction to the death of the man he and his expedition colleagues affectionately knew as 'The Boss.'

A ceasefire effectively brought to an end the Tan War on 11th July 1921 and talks continued between British and Irish representatives which led to the signing of the Anglo-Irish Treaty on 6th December 1921.

After a transitional period of one year, required after the signing of the treaty, and with Royal assent, the Irish Free State (*Saorstát Éireann*) came into existence on 6th December 1922; yet, its ratification only served to highlight the differences, as it was only narrowly passed by delegates of *Dáil Éireann*.

A day later, on 7th December 1922, Unionist MPs exercised their right under the terms of the treaty to opt out of the Irish Free State. In doing so, they partitioned six of the nine counties of Ulster which would remain under the governance of Britain.

It was this act of partition that gave rise, in June 1922, to what would become The Irish Civil War (*Cogadh Cathartha na hÉireann*).

It was a conflict that was fought between opposing sides to the treaty and one that would divide old comrades and family members who had fought together during the War of Independence.

Hostilities continued and would result in further casualties until it came to an end on 24th May 1923 when anti-treaty forces supported an order issued by their leadership to dump their arms.

Previous accounts of Crean's life have nurtured a popular belief that Tom Crean kept a low profile for fear of reprisals from Irish Nationalists because of his association with the British, but the evidence clearly points to a very different story.

On his return to Ireland after retirement, Crean was an active member of his community and among his close associates were prominent local members of the Volunteers who had fought against the Crown in the pre-treaty years.

In Annascaul, Robert Knightly, the train station master, as well as being Crean's closest friend was the 5th Battalion Kerry No.1 Brigade's Intelligence Officer during the Tan War. Knightly's commander, Patrick O'Neill, the Annascaul dentist, had, in 1921, been sentenced to 5 years penal servitude for his activities yet his political prisoner status had seen him released after the treaty had been signed.[26]

Both men, along with other former volunteers, were friends of Tom Crean and together in 1925, the three men were serving members of the Annascaul Coal Committee, where they helped distribute coal to the poor in the surrounding area.[27]

Coupled with the fact that a veteran of the Easter Rising wrote the first comprehensive account of Tom Crean's life, it casts huge doubt upon the perception that Tom Crean was alienated by Republicans for his service in the British Navy.

Among the witness statements later gathered and compiled by Ireland's Bureau of Military History Collection, was one confirming that British ex-soldiers and sailors living in and around Annascaul were in sympathy with the Republicans in their fight against the military and the Black and Tans.[28]

A number of ex-servicemen returning to their homeland during the Tan War revolted against their former employers after finding themselves, and their compatriots, to be among the oppressed. That they sympathised with those battling to break free from British rule at a time when daily atrocities were being carried out against their neighbours comes as no surprise.

It may well have been another factor in Crean declining the invitation of Shackleton to join his last expedition.

Little else is known of Tom Crean's political leanings; yet, it was reputed that he was later a supporter of Eamon De Valera's Fianna Fáil party which came into being in 1926.[29]

In troubled times, when the people of Ireland would continue to witness many victims of a bloody war, the distress for Tom Crean was no greater than through the troubled short life of his second child, Kate.

Born in 1920, Crean's child had known no respite from illnesses and it is known that Crean and his wife, Ellen, both of whom had a strong Catholic faith, took a decision to make the journey to the holy shrine of Lourdes in France. It had been widely recorded that the water flowing from the grotto, where the Virgin Mary was reputed to have appeared to a local girl, Bernadette Soubirous, in 1858, had miraculously cured a number of the sick who bathed in or drank from it, of their illnesses. Among the administrators organising the trip for pilgrims in Kerry, was the Annascaul parish priest Father T. J. Lyne and it is safe to deduce that Crean joined 5,000 of his compatriots on the second Irish National Pilgrimage to Lourdes.[30]

Before embarking on the pilgrimage, Tom Crean's mother, Catherine, died on 15th September 1924 and it was he who signed the death certificate.[31] She was 85 years old. The years since his retirement had not been kind to Crean and, despite his renowned mental strength, he was suffering blows far worse than the Antarctic blizzards could ever have thrown at him.

The death certificate records that his mother was a widow, although there is no evidence of the date of his father's passing. Tom Crean's marriage announcement did signify that Patrick Crean was present at his son's wedding in September 1917 and we can only guess the date of Patrick's passing. In the four year period since his retirement, Tom Crean had lost his brother, his mother and, possibly in the same period, his father.

Tragically, and less than two months later, on 8th December 1924, Tom Crean's young daughter Kate passed away.[32] Soon after returning from the pilgrimage, Kate's short life came to a premature end after a fatal bout of bronchopneumonia. For all his recent family losses, nothing could have prepared him for the devastating loss of a child and, coming shortly after the loss of his mother, it was a cruel turn of events that will have caused him grief beyond the comprehension of most.

Kate was the middle child of three daughters and having to deal with and overcome her loss must have been extremely painful for Crean. He had two other young daughters to care for, Mary and Eileen, and, with his wife, Nell, had to somehow summon the strength to continue.

Their continuing grief may have prompted the proposed sale of the pub in June 1926[33] and it was, again, put up for auction in January 1928[34] before being withdrawn in an apparent change of heart.

Although Tom Crean shied away from talking about his exploits in the navy and Antarctica, it did not prevent a number of visitors travelling from far and wide to reminisce and reacquaint themselves with the Irish Giant. One such visitor in March 1926 was Dan O'Sullivan, another Kerry native who had risen to become the Chief of Police of the Falkland Islands.[35] Dan was the first to greet Shackletonand Crean

Irish Independent 26th February 1920

As was his nature of avoiding the spotlight, Tom Crean can be seen here peering out behind Leonard Hussey, the banjo player, on the occasion of Shackleton's 100th lecture at the Philharmonic Hall, London. Shackleton is seated front left beside Frank Wild (centre) and Frank Worsley (sat right)

as they landed at Port Stanley on 31st May 1916 aboard the *Southern Sky* after the first failed attempt to rescue the men at Elephant Island. Another visit saw the nephew of Captain Scott make his way up to Annascaul after landing his plane on nearby Inch beach.[36] He, like others, was fully aware of the celebrity of the man they were there to see but the spotlight was never a place that Crean found comfort in and he shunned it without regret.

In 1929, after deciding to rebuild the pub which had hitherto been plagued by flooding from the nearby river,[37] the sign on the front elevation of the pub read South Pole Inn. It must have generated intrigue as to why it was so named. The title was clearly an open statement of his past life or, perhaps, an instance where homage to his friend and Terra Nova colleague, Edgar Evans, overrode his preference for privacy.

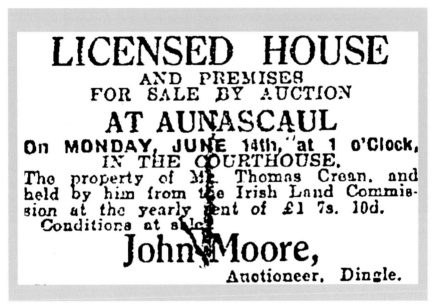

LICENSED HOUSE
AND PREMISES
FOR SALE BY AUCTION
AT AUNASCAUL
On MONDAY, JUNE 14th, at 1 o'Clock, IN THE COURTHOUSE.
The property of Mr. Thomas Crean, and held by him from the Irish Land Commission at the yearly rent of £1 7s. 10d.
Conditions at sale.
John Moore,
Auctioneer, Dingle.

Liberator 1st June 1926

Evans and Crean had known one another for 11 years and had formed a close bond, particularly while serving on their second expedition together aboard Terra Nova. It was during this expedition that Edgar had announced his intention to open a pub upon his return home. It seems very likely that Evans would have named it with reference to his expeditions to Antarctica as a place where visitors would be drawn in to visit the man who'd reached the South Pole with Scott.

When Tom Crean waved his friend good luck and farewell on his journey to the South Pole on January 4th 1912, little would he have imagined it being the last time he would ever see him alive. Crean would, though, see his friend's publican ambitions realised, not on the Gower Peninsula in Wales, birthplace and home of his lost friend, Edgar Evans, but on Ireland's Dingle Peninsula.

For Crean, the life of a publican was not quite as you'd expect and it was left to his wife Nell to work the bar while Tom would often walk the back roads calling in on his friends or relations. It was an arrangement that worked well as Nell had been reared in a public house a short distance from the South Pole Inn - one made famous in later years for its colourful frontage and its popular owner, Dan Foley. On days when the mood took him, Crean would sit chatting with patrons for hours. His presence and the thrill of being in his good company must have been a draw for those stepping through the doors of the South Pole Inn. One insight into the humour and wit of the 'Irish Giant' comes in the following tale:

One Friday morning, as the traders were heading down to Dingle from Tralee for the monthly cattle fair, the train broke down at Annascaul. Carrying their own food provisions for the weekend ahead, such as black puddings, sausages and bacon, a group of railwaymen and traders decided to use the downtime to head over to Crean's bar for a drink. It was a place where they knew the large kitchen could be utilised to rustle up a bite to eat.

Being a Catholic meant it was forbidden to eat meat on a Friday, yet Tom, being the accommodating host he was, took to the stove to rustle up a full Irish breakfast for his hungry guests. Soon enough, the aromas reached upstairs to Nell, Crean's wife, and she set about giving him an earful for his sacrilegious deeds on the holy day.

Crean, unmoved by his chastisement, carried on with his sinful deed and quickly retorted, *"Friday be damned, if I had a skelp of your arse, I'd have eaten that too where I'd been."*[38]

It was a reply typical of Tom Crean's wit and humour which played such a vital role, on a number of occasions, in keeping up the spirits of his Antarctic colleagues when all seemed lost.

Dr Edward Wilson, known as 'Uncle Bill' to his expedition colleagues and one of the fateful five who never made it back from the South Pole with Scott, summed Crean up well, stating, *"He was a delightful creature."*[39]

Crean's brother, Daniel, who still lived and farmed the land with his wife, Margaret, at the Gortacurraun townland where Tom was born, died aged 55, on 3rd June 1932, after contracting encarditis, a rare infection of the heart. It was another loss Crean must have felt deeply and he was present at the death of the brother he visited often.[40]

For much of his time in retirement and after the wars, Tom Crean led a quiet and largely uneventful life, running the pub with his wife while bringing up his daughters.

In an interview given in 2000, Crean's eldest daughter Mary revealed how Tom was an avid boxing fan and would often pair together pensioners in fun-filled, mock match-ups when they called to the South Pole Inn after collecting their payments on a Friday.[41]

What ignited the fun and games was Crean's huge admiration for the Cork boxer, Jack Doyle, who was later famed as much for his singing ability as his boxing skills. On 12th July 1933, Doyle was given the opportunity to fight for the British title fighting against the Welshman Jack Petersen at White City Stadium, London.

The fight sparked huge interest in Ireland where Doyle, a celebrity of the day, had generated a huge army of fans after a rapid rise up the heavyweight ranks. Across Ireland crowded rooms and bars sat in silence around their transistor radio's only to hear the referee end their dreams of a famous victory.

Doyle, known as the 'Gorgeous Gael' entered the ring in front of a sell-out 60,000 crowd and after smashing Petersen with a number of successive low blows was disqualified after two rounds.

Doyle's purse of £3,000 was withheld yet he won it back via the courts before heading off to America to seek further fame in the movies.

As comfortable as he was to talk about a variety of interests, such as sports or his love of gardening, Tom Crean retired from talking about his life as an explorer. Many believe this was because he served the British, the same power who had employed the Black and Tans to brutally uphold their authority on the people of Ireland. His reticence to speak of his past could also have been due to the fact that very few people on the planet could ever truly understand what a human had to endure in the most inhospitable place on earth. The overriding reason, from what we know of his character, is that to talk of his exploits would have been considered by him as bragging - and bragging was not part of his makeup.

In remembering Crean, it's important to explore beyond the tales of his heroism. Tom Crean had the ability to raise the spirits of others in the harshest and bleakest of environments when morale can rapidly decline. He used humour, song and wit as tools to inspire others at a time and a turn of events when they most needed it. But Crean's sensitivity and compassion extended beyond that shown to his fellow human beings. Iconic as the image is of toughness staring steely-eyed into the camera, wearing a twin-peaked polar hat and with his pipe held firmly through gritted teeth, there was another side to the Irish Giant - that of animal lover.

Crean loved animals in a time long before animal rights and our protection of them were commonplace. He was a man ahead of his time in many ways. Even though his expeditions sometimes called for horses and dogs to be put down for the survival of the crew, it was a task that must have played havoc with Crean's emotions. Any loss of life was devastating to a man whose stock-in-trade was saving them.

After his return to retirement in Annascaul, part of his routine was walking the beautiful hillsides of his beloved County Kerry. These were journeys he undertook daily with his two dogs, Fido and Toby. On fine evenings, Crean would often walk the dogs down by nearby Bunaneer, a small seaside cove that is accessed via a road that slopes down to the sea. One particular evening, one of the dogs became victim of an unfortunate fate, falling to its death from the hillside; Crean scrambled down the road to the shingle beach, yet he could do nothing to save the dog. He was left inconsolable with grief as he wept and mourned its passing.[42]

The above tale was one recalled by John Knightly, who, as well as being the son of Crean's best friend, Annascaul stationmaster, Robert Knightly, was Tom's godson. Although John passed away in 2013, he left a wonderful legacy in the form of recorded interviews undertaken by Tralee oral historians, Maurice and Jane O'Keefe. One of these interviews concentrates on his memories of Tom Crean and his recollections not only provide us with gems of information but they offer us a first-hand account and a greater insight into Crean's life after retirement.

John, who left Annascaul to teach in Cashel, County Tipperary, described Crean as a real character and the man he, along with other children in the village, knew as 'Funny Crean.' Every evening, he recalled, Tom Crean would call to Annascaul railway station to collect his newspaper. The papers would arrive on the train from Tralee, which often arrived late due to the incoming tide preventing its journey from Blennerville.

Delays were unimportant, as they gave Crean and his stationmaster friend, Knightly, time to catch up with one another and, in the small office, they would chat away.

A Headmistress and Girl Pat's Skipper

'Captain Orsborne, skipper of *Girl Pat,* was held up as an example for girls by Miss Steel, headmistress of the Worcester Secondary Girls' School at the prize distribution yesterday.

Deploring the unwillingness of girls *"to leave home or to venture to anything beyond the nearest office or cash box"*, she said:

"Such girls might with advantage, read and take to heart the story of the spirited performance of the skipper of the Girl Pat, who, whatever his critics may think about him, at any rate, had the imagination and pluck to do something unusual and adventurous well away from the home port."

Belfast Newsletter, July 29th August, 1936

In April 1936, a news story was gathering pace around the world of a seaman, George Orsborne, who (according to reports) "in a fit of madness" had taken a trawler, *Girl Pat,* out from Grimsby. Instead of heading for the nearest North Sea fishing grounds to gather the weekly catch for his employers, Orsborne informed his small crew of four that they were going on a little adventure.[43] The saga made headlines around the world, as the little adventure morphed into a round-the-world trip followed every step of the way by the newspapers and, in turn, by an enthralled public keeping tabs on the "mad seaman." On 19th June 1936, the trawler, *Girl Pat*, was eventually recovered in Georgetown, the port and capital of Guyana, South America, after what was described as "an exciting two-hour chase."[44] Osborne was arrested and imprisoned for 18 months for theft of the vessel.[45] The stolen trawler had spent ten weeks at sea and had covered over 5,000 miles in her unauthorised world cruise. It was an escapade that captured the imagination of a sympathetic public who revelled in the romanticism of the anti-establishment hero captain.

More than most, sea-going expert Tom Crean took a particular delight in the story as he pointed out on the world map, pinned on Knightly's office wall, the places where Orsborne should avoid or coastal areas he should pay special attention to. Robert Knightly was left mightily impressed by Crean's knowledge of the world's seas and oceans and by his rooting for the maverick underdog. The empathy shown to Orsborne by Crean is an interesting insight into the character of a man who had served under the strict discipline of the navy, where such behaviour and disobedience would never be tolerated.

In an ironic footnote to the story, it was reported that another Hull trawler skipper, who may have been familiar with *Girl Pat* and its maverick captain, volunteered his services to bring the vessel back from Georgetown. Sailing the trawler over 4,500 miles back to Grimsby would take considerable skill and expertise. His offer was declined by the authorities but he would have been more than up to the task after his experience of a journey far more hazardous. The volunteer happened to be Crean's former colleague aboard *Endurance* and *James Caird*, John Vincent.[46]

Girl Pat was refitted and returned home under the ownership of Girl Pat Ltd, the brainchild of two young Grimsby trawlerman who proposed to bring her back via the same globetrotting route she made under her former skipper Orsborne. To man the small vessel on her journey home, they advertised for a crew *"seeking an adventure."*

It's clear that young John Knightly had a close relationship with Crean and he refers frequently to Crean's sense of fun. On another occasion, John recalls his father Bob and Tom Crean being concerned as to the welfare of a friend they'd not seen for some days: Matty, a former soldier from Maum, the area that leads up out of Annascaul village towards the beach at Inch. It was decided that they should pay Matty a visit and John accompanied his father and godfather to Matty's house. On reaching the house, Tom hit the door a great few rattles and proclaimed in a loud voice, *"Open up in the King's Name."* Poor Matty, who had been spending a few days laid up in bed unwell, hurried to the door covered in feathers. Springing out of the bed to answer what he assumed were the authorities, he had burst his old mattress. Needless to say, there were howls of laughter at the fun of it all.[47]

Crean's sense of mischievousness had also not been lost on John's mother, Crean's cousin, who would lock the door if she saw him approaching the house of an evening for fear she would never be able to settle the children to sleep if Tom kept them up with further frivolities.

The accounts of all who knew him - his expedition leaders, his fellow crew members, his family and his village neighbours - offers us an insight into the character of the man. Crean was tough, humorous, sensitive and loyal. He was an extraordinary man who did extraordinary things.

Having travelled the world and been involved in so many dramas, adapting to life back home in Ireland never seemed to trouble Crean, despite the turbulent times he returned to.

People warmed to him and not just because of his reputation and achievements but because he was likeable and fun.

People would also have been aware that a steadfast mindset that served him through his expeditions was a major facet of Crean's character. The following story about him indicates just this.

Minor squabbles that, today, are invariably over and done with in the exchange of a few words were, for Ireland in Tom Crean's lifetime, often settled in the courtrooms. In the 19th century and up to the 1920s, they were titled *Petty Sessions*. In their early format, these were sittings that judged people for the most minor offences, such as drunkenness, livestock trespass or damage to a neighbour's hedge. Fines were levied upon the party found at fault by the Magistrates who were made up, in the main, of landowners and agents.

Petty Sessions later gave rise to the local Courts where similar quarrels of the time were played out.

It was in sessions such as these that we can glean a further glimpse into Tom Crean's mindset in his later life.

Crean was a keen gardener and kept his land in good order.

It's easy to see how anyone spoiling his work would have incurred his wrath. After all, if, as the expression has it, 'an Englishman's home is his castle', then I would venture that 'an Irishman's land is his soul.'

In 1930, a Judge at Annascaul threw out a case Crean brought against a neighbour after a series of minor altercations that included reports of "*trespass, damage to hedges, and a charge of abusive language.*"[48] The same neighbour brought a similar case against Crean in 1933[49] and so the charges went back and forth in a series of events that led the exasperated judge to suggest the parish priest in Annascaul be instructed to settle the matter.

John Knightly's recollections of Crean perhaps give us another understanding of the dispute with Tom's rival. He recalled, with great amusement:

> "*I remember an occasion where another man over at the top of the village having cabbage plants or something similar and, in early summer, Tom was digging the potatoes and he wasn't great friends at all with this other man and he sent me over. 'Would you have a go at him and get 50 cabbage plants?' and, so, I went over and the other man said to me 'Who're these for, sure, I thought your dad hadn't any garden yet?' 'They're for Funny Crean', I said, 'Well, I'm not giving him any' came the terse reply.*"

To howls of laughter, John ends the story:

"So, I went home without the plants for Tom."

We are left to wonder whether Crean's gardener adversary is one and the same person who had been his courtroom rival on numerous occasions.

Crean's sense of order, a remnant of his naval upbringing, was again brought to mind by John as he recalls Tom being very methodical. One example of this was how Crean used to tie up sticks he had gathered for firewood in little bundles and stack them neatly on shelves in an outside shed in readiness to collect and start up the fire.

Having spent most of his life in the navy, Crean's life after retiring from the service was understandably regimented and it transpires, from his godson's recollections, that this remained throughout his time at home in Annascaul.

The influence of a life spent in close proximity to the sea was strong and, if ever a fine evening allowed him the opportunity, he would walk down to the coast at Bunaneer and gaze out at the horizon and think of a time beyond it. The world's seas and oceans were always in his blood.

On occasion, he would take the train down to Dingle and catch up with friends. One such friend was Dick McDonnell and, today, the pub he owned, *Dick Macks*, is one of many to be found in this colourful and welcoming seaside fishing town.

Some years ago, when chatting over a drink with Dick's son, Oliver, he recounted that, even on the warmest of days, the returned explorer Crean wore an overcoat.

It's little wonder, given the below freezing conditions his frame had been exposed to after spending much of his navy career in Antarctica. It's as if he had literally become 'chilled to the bone.'

Today, outside Dick Mack's pub, a commemoration of celebrities and famous names who've visited the iconic pub over the years take up their own star carving in the pavement outside. Among the first to be laid down by Oliver was in tribute to his father's friend, Tom Crean, who was a hero to Kerry folk before the world was able to read his story.

One can only imagine the aches and pains that Crean will have suffered as he lived out the final years of his life. Such was his character that he would never have openly complained about them.

More than one story, passed down by those who knew him in the locality of Annascaul, recounts how Tom Crean would often wash his feet in the stream that runs adjacent to the *South Pole Inn*.

The accounts of those who were children at the time, recalled how blackened his feet and toes were and that they were sworn to secrecy, by their friend 'Funny Crean', never to tell anyone. Fortunately, for Crean, Annascaul had several shoemakers to cater for his troublesome feet. It was shoemaker, James Sayers, a distant relative of the great Peig Sayers, who had the task of making the specially designed boots before delivering them personally to Tom at the South Pole Inn. His sore feet were, of course, a result of the thousands of miles he'd trekked over Antarctica's hostile landscape. Crean had, in fact, covered more distance than either Scott or Shackleton over the course of his southern expeditions.

Just over a year before his death, Tom Crean travelled to Cork in May 1937 for the christening of his grand-niece, Norah Mary Joan, daughter of his nephew, Willie Crean. He was there in his role of godfather to the grandchild of his brother, Cornelius, who he had lost to the War of Independence 17 years earlier.[50]

Over the course of his life, Tom Crean had displayed an unswerving loyalty to family, friends and expedition leaders, and this had seen him travel many thousands of miles across the world. The short 70-mile journey to Cork was one he would make again just over a year later, yet it would be his last.

TWO KERRY TRAVELL ERS MEET

Liberator
23rd March 1926

The visit of Mr. Daniel J. O'Sullivan to his native Kerry, and to the Aunascaul district, led to his meeting his erstwhile friend, Tom Crean, the intrepid antartic traveller.

The meeting of those two travellers in the quiet and calm of Aunascaul life was a rare opportunity to discuss their earlier meeting under the Southern skies.

It was an anxious time in the lives of Sir Ernest Shackleton, Capt. Wolseley and Tom Crean, when they bid farewell to their comrades on the icebound shores of Elephant Island, and set sail in a small boat to seek relief in order that all might not perish. Landing in an obscure corner of the Faulklands, away from the haunts of men, they had to abandon their frail craft and with scanty raiment and no food, trudge their way over the snow covered cliffs and ravines of this desolate island. On reaching Stanley they were given a kindly Irish welcome by Mr. O'Sullivan. His kindness to those weary travellers on the occasion is sure to last while the vital spark remains.

Mr. O'Sullivan has made many friends during his stay here who, with a sigh, will wish him bon voyage when he returns to his home.

(DANL. FOLEY).

IRISH NATIONAL PILGRIMAGE TO LOURDES.

SIGNAL HONOUR FOR BISHOP OF KERRY.

Tuesday.

The main body of the pilgrims to Lourdes left yesterday. The Kerry contingent of pilgrims and invalids are under the charge of Very Rev. T. J. Lyne, Diocesan Manager and Secretary of the Pilgrimage. We understand his Lordship Most Rev. Charles O'Sullivan, D.D., Lord Bishop of Kerry; the Right Rev. Monsignor O'Leary, P.P., V.G., Dean of Kerry, and several of the Kerry clergy have already arrived at Lourdes. His Lordship the Bishop of Kerry has been assigned the signal honour of singing the first High Mass at Lourdes, which opens the pilgrimage. There are about 30,000 Associates of the pilgrimage in Kerry. In St. John's Church, Tralee, large numbers received Holy Communion at the morning Masses, and big congregations attend the evening Lourdes devotions, which will last until the end of the pilgrimage, Friday, 10th October. Thousands of men, women and children in Tralee are wearing the Lourdes badges. A temporary altar has been placed in St. John's Church, in front of the High Altar, on which is a statue of Our Lady of Lourdes with Bernadette at her feet. The altar is beautifully decorated with flowers and lighted with multi-coloured tiny electric lamps, opposite which from early morning to late at night devout worshippers kneel in prayerful supplication.

Liberator
4th October 1924

> *What you leave behind is not what is engraved in stone monuments but what is woven into the lives of others*

Pericles

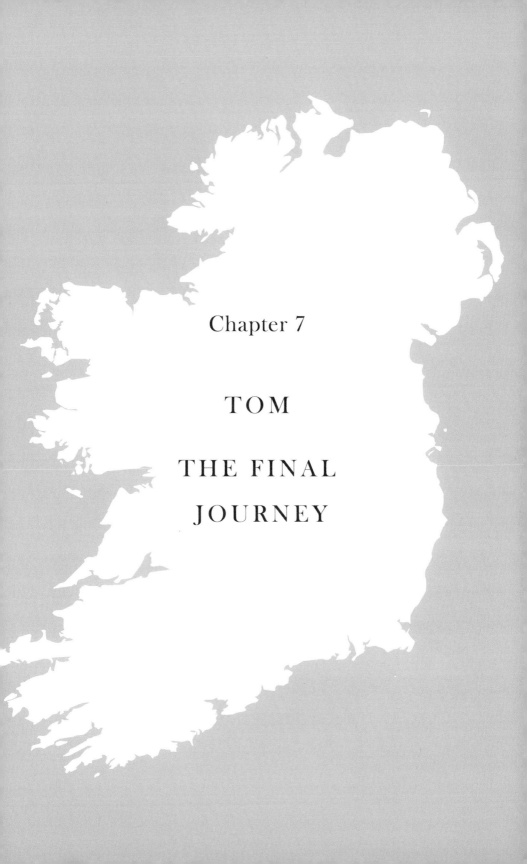

Chapter 7

TOM

THE FINAL

JOURNEY

In the spring of 1938, the most senior officer in the British Navy, Admiral of the Fleet and 12th Earl of Cork and Orrery, William Boyle, was on vacation staying at Dingle while spending much of his holiday fishing the rivers of Annascaul.[1]

Not far from where he would be casting his line into the waters, a man who had felt compelled to leave the same area to join the navy some 45 years earlier was entering the final months of his life.

Crean was suffering from a burst appendix and, if treated quickly, it would have been a routine procedure enabling a relatively quick recovery without any long-term effects.

However, the danger of contracting peritonitis, if a burst appendix is not attended to quickly, can prove fatal.

No doctor capable of undertaking the operation was available in the Tralee hospital he attended and, so, he was transferred via ambulance on a 70-mile journey to Cork's Bon Secour hospital where, finally, his appendix was removed.

Because the operation had been delayed, an infection had developed and, after a week in the hospital, the unheralded hero of three major

Antarctic expeditions contracted peritonitis.

On 27th July 1938, Tom Crean died. In a sad twist of fate, when his own hour of need arrived, there was no one available with the life-saving skills he himself had displayed on many occasions.

His funeral was the largest Annascaul had ever witnessed as his family, neighbours, friends, dignitaries and a number of former naval colleagues bade farewell to the Irish Giant.

Tom Crean was laid to rest in a family tomb he had built with his own hands in Ballinacourty cemetery, close to Annascaul and not far from his Gortacurraun birthplace.

The inscription on the side of his tomb reads 'Home is the Sailor, Home from the Sea.' On top of Crean's stone coffin sits a ceramic bowl of flowers, sent by Lieutenant Teddy Evans. It remains there still today and serves as a timeless reminder of the debt of gratitude owed to a man who, on a number of documented occasions, had put the lives of others above his own.

Lieutenant Evans, who, by this time, had been promoted to Admiral Mountevans, owed his life to Tom Crean and he never forgot the historic solo march Crean undertook to save his life, expressing a love for the Irish Giant.

The card attached to his floral tribute read:

"In affectionate remembrance from an Antarctic Comrade."[2]

Tom Crean was buried still wearing, around his neck, the holy scapular that he had worn throughout his life. His strong faith, it seems, had seen him through a host of perilous and historic journeys most ordinary humans could not have survived.

Certain people deserve a pass to immortality and the world is a poorer place without them. Tom Crean was such a man.

STORY OF EPIC RESCUE IN POLAR WASTES

(By George N. Gormley.)

IN the little graveyard at Ballin-courtry, Co. Kerry, there was laid to rest, yesterday, one who nobly contributed his share to the part which Ireland and Irishmen have played in the making of world history.

He was Thomas Crean, of Annascaul, Co. Kerry, ex-Petty Officer, R.N. Of tremendous physique, Crean saw

Mr. Thomas Crean.

service with three Polar Expeditions—twice with Scott and once with Shackleton.

It was the heroic part he took in Capt. Scott's ill-fated 1910 Expedition which made him one of the outstanding figures in that gallant party which set out on the Terra Nova from New Zealand, and which prompted Admiral F. R. G. R. Evans, R.N., to dedicate his book, "South with Scott," to Crean.

Those of us who are old enough read daily at the time the story of that epic struggle in the barren wastes; of the hunger, sickness, and the unselfishness in comradeship where each and every one risked their lives by acts of heroism that each might live, no one excelled Crean in the heroic part he played in all this.

750 MILES TREK.

On January 4, 1912, when the main party—Capt. Scott, Dr. E. A. Wilson, Capt. G. E. Oates, and Seaman Evans, with the supporting party—Admiral (then Lieut.) Evans, Lieut. H. R. Bowers, P.O. Thomas Crean; and Stoker Lashly, were 146 geographical miles from the Pole—a matter of 11 or 12 days' good sledging—Scott decided to take his own team with the addition of Bowers to the Pole.

Provisions were running short and it was the supply of food that decided Scott to cut down the party.

With a shake-hands all round, Admiral Evans,

Crean and Lashly, the last to see Scott and his four companions alive, turned to face the 750-miles-trek-

back to the base, taking with them only four days' provisions.

FIGHT FOR LIFE.

"No man," wrote Admiral Evans of Crean and Lashly, "was better served by these two men."

It was a fight for life. Day after day they fought their way over the high Polar tableland. The silence was ghastly, and navigational difficulties made it impossible to keep direction. The blizzards which lasted for days blinded and baffled them and often sent them wide of their course.

The little party heroically battled on until Admiral Evans was stricken with scurvy. He entreated his two companions to leave him and struggle on, but instead they lashed him on the sledge and forced on until at last through hunger and fatigue they had to give up.

They erected their little tent and placed Admiral Evans inside. Crean and Lashly discussed the situation. There was only one thing for it—help must be got. Hut Point, one of the bases, was 35 miles away, and Crean, leaving Lashly to nurse Admiral Evans, and bidding the latter farewell, set off on his journey to Hut Point. He took no food with him—only a few biscuits and a bar of chocolate.

RAN INTO BLIZZARD

Days passed and, with no sign of help arriving, all hope in the little tent was abandoned.

Crean had not covered many miles when he ran into a blizzard.

With his folded arms acting as a shield, and staggering about in a stooping position, he had lost direction. How many miles he had covered he could not say, but he estimated that he circled fifty. Eventually he reached his destination, but, so blinding was the blizzard, that he tottered past the tent at Hut Point.

Dr. E. L. Atkinson, who was inside, saw the dark form fall past the tent door and rushed out. He led the exhausted Crean inside.

When the latter, with the aid of a stimulant, had sufficiently recovered to tell of his mission, Dr. Atkinson and the dog-boy, Dimitri, hastily harnessed a sledge and set off hot-foot. In six hours they were back at Hut Point with the patient and Lashly, and Crean and his companions were safely reunited once more.

DECORATED.

When the expedition reached England, Crean was given the Albert Medal by the King for his brave act in helping his companions to win through. May he rest in peace.

Irish Independent 29th July 1938

179

Late Mr. Tom Crean R.N., Aunascaul.

Deep and widespread regret is felt at the untimely and unexpected demise of Warrant Officer Tom Crean, R.N., retired, of Polar fame, which occured on July 27th at the Bon Secour Home, Cork. The funeral took place next day, after Solemn Requiem Mass, from the Church of the Secret Heart, Annascaul, to Ballinacurty graveyard, which lies sheltered across the hill separating it from the homestead where he first saw the light some sixty years ago.

As a tribute to the popularity in which he was held, he was borne to the graveyard, a distance of nearly two miles, on the shoulders of Naval Comrades and neighbours, many of whom were his schoolboy contemporaries. The cortege, representative of every class of the community, was one of the largest ever seen in the district, and, as it wended its mournful way, many were the expressions of sorrow given vent to at the passing of a stalwart, who was a kindly neighbour and a good friend.

The celebrant at the Solemn Requiem was Rev. J. McGrath, Adm.; deacon, Rev. J. F. Kennedy; sub-deacon, Rev. P. Kennedy, who also pronounced the final Absolution.

The chief mourners were:—Widow (Mrs. E. Crean), Mary and Eileen (daughters); W. Crean and Margaret Crean, Cork; Hugh and Mary Crean, John and Michael Devane and sisters, and Mrs. M. Galvin, Annascaul (nephews and nieces); Mrs. B. Foley, Mrs. K. Leyne and Mrs. N. Pigott (sisters-in-law); W. J. Pigott (brother-in-law); P. Foley, Curran family, Kennedy family and Moriarty family, Annalack; Galvin family, Gurticurrane; Courtney family and Kennedy family, Ballinacurty and Coumduff; Miss J. Kennedy, Eugene and Mrs. Moriarty, Mrs. Devane, D. Courtney, Crean family, Ballinasare; D. Crean, District Court Clerk, Tralee; John and Mrs. Moriarty, Caherslee, do.; John and Mrs. O'Sullivan, The Basin, do.; Ed. Crean, Ashe family, Post Office, Denis and Mary Sullivan, Annascaul (relatives); Bob and Mrs. Knightly, Banteer.

Prayers at the graveside were recited by Rev. J. McGrath, Adm., assisted by Rev. P. Kennedy and Rev. J. Kennedy. Also present: Very Rev. T. J. Canon Lyne, Dingle; Rev. J. Slattery, Killarney; Rev. Fr. Casey do.; Rev. Fr. Moriarty, Inch; Rev. Fr Landers, Ballarat; Rev. T. Kennedy, Melbourne; Rev. M. J. Kennedy, London; Rev. Fr. Houlihan and Rev. Fr. O'Connor.

Mass Cards:—From Widow and Daughters; Mrs. B. Foley and family, Annascaul; Mrs. K. Leyne, do.; Ashe family, Post Office, do.; Miss Joan Hayes, do.; Mrs. N. Pigott and family, Dublin; Misses Alice and Floss Martin, do.; Matthew Sweeney, do.; Montie and Austin Martin, do.; O'Brien family, Princes Street, Tralee; Mrs. A. Martin, Ashe Street, do.; Miss A. Nunan, Ballymullen, do.; Bob and Mrs. Knightly, Banteer; Mrs. Moriarty, Castletownbere.

Floral tributes included a wreath from Admiral Sir E. R. G. R. Evans—"In affectionate remembrance from an Antarctic Comrade."

Messages of sympathy were received from:—Commander O'Connell, R.N., Knight of Malta, Killarney; Professor J. Pigott, B.A., H.Dip.Ed., Dublin; P. Pigott, junior, do.; Mr. and Mrs. Gormley, do.; Montie and Austin Martin, do.; C. J. Downing, solicitor, Tralee; Com. O'Neill, do.; Mrs. O'Sullivan, The Palace, Killarney; Mrs. Moriarty, Castletownbere; Sean Crean, Urlingford; John Moore, Dingle; Messrs. Goggin and Foley, do.; Mrs B. O'Sullivan, Caherciveen; Messrs. M. D. Daly & Co., Ltd., Cork; Messrs. Clune & Co., Ltd., Limerick.

Mrs. Crean, daughters and relatives, wish to return sincere thanks to all those who sympathised with them in their recent sad bereavement, sent Mass cards, telegrams and letters of sympathy, and those who called and attended the funeral, and trust this will be accepted by all in grateful acknowledgment.

The tomb where Tom Crean was laid to rest in the Ballinacourty cemetery a short distance from where he drew his first breath.

It remains a place of pilgrimage for Crean's admirers who visit from all comers of the world to pay homage to an extraordinary man.

The stones and pebbles on top of the tomb are placed there as a mark of respect and surround the bowl of flowers sent by Admiral Mountevans, one of the many men whose lives he saved.

66

The secret of change is to focus all of your energy not on fighting the old but on building the new

---

99

Socrates

Chapter 8

THE LEGACY
AND THE CAMPAIGN

Less than a year after the death of Tom Crean, the Second World War broke out and, for the following six years, there was very little newspaper space given over to the feats and accomplishments of polar exploration.

Independent Ireland was a country still in its infancy and it was not until June 1949 that Crean's name resurfaced. His widow, Ellen, travelled by special invitation to Cork where she met with her late husband's former *Terra Nova* colleague, Robert Forde, at the premier of the film *Scott of the Antarctic*.[1]

The film, as expected, focused on the race to reach the South Pole and on the fate of Captain Scott and his companions on their return. Consequently, the Tom Crean character was a given a very minor role with no reference to his historic life-saving march.

In the 1950s, a few newspaper articles recalled his heroics but the story of Crean still remained firmly under the radar.[2,3] Interestingly, it wasn't a mainstream article but a memorable account entitled *Polar Crean*, written by Denis Barry in The Capuchin Annual of 1952, that later alerted me to the story of a man born in a place I knew well.[4]

The back story behind this account of Crean's exploits is as illuminating as the story itself, as Denis Barry happened to be a pseudonym. The real name of the man responsible for writing the first comprehensive narrative of Tom Crean's time in Antarctica was Tadhg Gahan.

On 24th April 1916, the day that Tom Crean jumped aboard the *James Caird* to help bring about a seemingly impossible rescue, events were unfolding in his homeland, Ireland, that would enter the history books for a very different reason.

Irish republicans had taken over a number of strategic locations as the Easter Rising got underway. In one of these locations, the Jacobs biscuit factory, Tadhg Gahan, then a young Dublin student, would take up arms under the command of Thomas McDonagh, one of the seven signatories of the Proclamation of the Irish Republic (*Forógra na Poblachta*).

Tadhg played an active role in helping to fortify the factory against the expected attack of the British forces but the Jacobs complex was spared much of the onslaught that was taking place in Dublin's city centre.[5]

McDonagh and two other leaders at the biscuit factory, Major John McBride and Michael O'Hanrahan, would later be among sixteen men executed by the British in the aftermath of the rebellion that would, after two further conflicts, lead to the birth of a new nation.

For his part in the Easter Rising, Tadhg was imprisoned at Frongoch internment camp in Wales.

Later, while working as a journalist, Tadhg would write a novel under another pseudonym, 'Dermot Barry.' The book, *The Tuppence Ha'penny*, was a short novel based on the experiences of a young Dubliner through his schooldays up to the Easter Rising and ending with the Tan War. The book, which, it appears, was partly autobiograph-ical, was awarded the Tailteann Gold Medal for Literature in 1928. In the exalted company of William Butler Yeats and George Bernard Shaw, two other Tailteann award winners in the same year, Tadhg Gahan's achievement placed him on a respected literary platform.[6]

In 1931, the book was published and retitled *Tom Creagan*. Whether the renaming was a nod in admiration to Crean is anyone's guess but it is an interesting fact that a man who wrote the first de-finitive story about Tom Crean's time in Antarctica in 1952, should rename his book in this way.[7]

For over a century Tom Crean's contribution to Polar history has never been officially recognised by his country. Perhaps those elected representatives, who are enthralled by his feats, stop short of calling for his national recognition because they believe it may not prove popular with the electorate. Perhaps some consider Crean's de-cision to join the British Navy as an indication of 'disloyalty' rather than an act of survival for himself and his family in what were desper-ate times. A fresh look at Crean's timeline and circumstances, will, I hope, serve to redress that opinion.

Given the longstanding indifference in political circles for the case to honour Tom Crean, when a veteran of the Easter Rebellion such as Tadhg Gahan saw fit to write in fulsome praise of the Kerry man, it re-affirms that Tom Crean was as patriotic an Irishman as any other.

Gahan's admiration for Crean is clear from the outset of his story as he states:

"He was a simple bluejacket but his courage, strength and calm-ness in the gap of danger rank him high in the chronicles."

It is possible that Gahan and Crean were familiar with one another and the closing lines of *Polar Crean* may suggest so. It would also explain why Gahan's account was so thorough and well researched. In summarising Crean's life after retirement he writes that Crean:

".........settled down in Annascaul, talking Irish as if he had never been away. Despite the hardships he had endured and the wounds they left, he never lost his fine spirit and cheery disposition and he was a kindly neighbour and a good friend. People came from far to see him and about his house were many tokens of his fame, but he was modest enough about his exploits."

Sadly, Tadhg Gahan's account never gained the audience or the traction it deserved but today with a host of additional information to hand about Crean, Gahan's account can be read with new eyes.

In the decades to follow, the stories of his leaders were celebrated in books and on the screen while Tom Crean's part in their sagas still went largely unheralded. A television series, *The Last Place on Earth*, in 1985, focused on Scott and Amundsen's race for the pole in a TV adaptation that, again, featured Crean in a blink-and-you-miss-him role.

Tom Crean never did make the transition to the commissioned ranks but an Annascaul neighbour of Crean's, James Kennedy, did.

Born in 1862 at Ballynacourty, Kennedy had taken the same journey as Tom some 15 years earlier, joining up as a Boy 2nd class aboard *HMS Impregnable* in 1878. In 1912, Kennedy was promoted to the rank of Lieutenant and, after 42 years' service, he retired a Lieutenant Commander on 26th August 1920. It had been a remarkable rise for a man who, like Crean, had left his homeland in search of better fortune.[8]

His had been a familiar face and voice that offered boys from his homeland a valued crumb of comfort as they entered their harsh new lives aboard the training ship.

It is extremely likely that Crean knew Kennedy before he entered the navy - they may even have been related; and, over his period of tenure in the navy, Crean formed a close bond with his commander. They remained lifelong friends and Kennedy was among the very few people that Crean wrote to during his lifetime.

One such letter written by Crean on 26th February 1912, reveals James to have been willing to act as a marriage broker. In it Crean states:

"I am very thankful to you for what you have done for me regarding myself and Hannah. I hope to God things will turn out all right. I must thank you very much James for being so good as to break the subject with her father, any how I am glad I am in the bidding and with the help of God we shall have a time at the wedding please God."

Just a week after his historic lifesaving march, Crean's mind was clearly set on his future and his return to Annascaul as he penned the letter to his great friend.

James died in 1943, five years after his protégé, Tom Crean, and, in 1985, Kennedy's daughter announced that she was putting two letters, written to her father by her godfather Tom Crean, up for auction. After an appeal for donations to purchase the letters proved successful, today they are contained within a box in County Kerry Museum.[9]

Addressed to his commanding officer, Lieutenant J.P. Kennedy, the letters also give Tom Crean's account of his exploits in Antarctica while serving on the ill-fated *Terra Nova* expedition. 1987 saw the opening of the Tom Crean Expedition at Dingle Library and the un-veiling of a commemorative plaque at the *South Pole Inn*, his former home.[10] The year also saw a proposal to name a square after him in Tralee, the county town of Kerry, but it failed to materialise.[11]

Among the journalists who did present a case for Crean's greater recognition was the writer and historian, Ryle Dwyer. Ryle's articles, unlike previous accounts of Crean's story, were among the first to question why this remarkable man had not been recognised and he made the point that such honour would have been bestowed upon him had he been of the officer class. Perhaps Ryle's thought-provoking ac-counts sowed the seeds for a resurgence of interest in the Tom Crean story that took place in the 1990s and beyond.[12]

The year 2000 saw the publication of Michael Smith's biogra-phy on Tom Crean and 2002 marked the year that the Guinness com-pany chose Tom Crean as the subject in what became a popular TV advert for the famous stout.

A one-man play about Crean, *Tom Crean - Antarctic Explorer*, written and performed by Aidan Dooley, also took to the stage in 2002, generating great reviews, as it still does today.

Again, in 2002, Sir Edmund Hilary was invited to Tralee to open an Antarctic Exhibition featuring a number of Tom Crean ar-tefacts[13] and, in the following year, a privately funded bronze statue, erected facing Tom's former home, the *South Pole Inn*, and created by sculptor Eamon O'Doherty, was unveiled by Crean's daughters, Mary and Eileen. Speaking at the ceremony, Marie Kennedy, chairperson of the committee set up to raise funds for the statue, said:

"It's wonderful that he's finally recognised in his home village. He's a local, national and international hero."[14]

Great commemorations though these all were for an Irish Hero, none resulted in a call for his official recognition.

The Tom Crean story was certainly gaining traction but it seemed to progress no further than a nod of approval or a nudge of acknowledgement for *"good old Tom."* Although the story was making great headway with a wider public, it was not connecting with the politicians and the decision-makers who had the power to finally provide official recognition to this great Irish hero. Sadly, that's been the case for Tom Crean ever since - his story was increasing in popularity but any progress beyond this would be entirely dependent on an appetite for recognition from within Ireland's corridors of power.

This injustice and a chance conversation with my brother, Mike Foley, who compared the naming of *Robin Hood Airport* after a fictional character to the lack of any recognition for the great Tom Crean, spurred me on to start a campaign to try and achieve official recognition for him as a national Irish hero.

So, in 2010, I created a Facebook members group believing that a digital campaign would generate a greater reach. I named the group *Kerry Airport Should Be Renamed Tom Crean Airport* and, although fans of the ambition were joining up in agreement, progress in a Facebook group at the time was limited, as fans had to apply for membership.

To dampen my resolve further, at the time, it became clear to me that not everyone agreed that Tom Crean was not being honoured sufficiently. Among the reasons cited was that Crean's story is now a part of the national curriculum in Irish schools.

However, I was aware that, when Irish children left school, they probably heard or saw nothing more about the hero whose story they had grown up with. What the small group in disagreement with me also failed to see, I determined, was that there were millions of people who had already left school knowing little or nothing of the Crean story.

And, so, in April 2014, I created a Facebook page to allow a wider reach. The numbers grew steadily. The page was attracting the attention of more Crean fans and, a Tralee native Eddie Barrett, a fan of Crean, offered to help out with posts to the page. Eddie's knowledge of Kerry was helpful, as was the fact that he was a shareholder in the airport. For almost two years, the focus was on a name change for Tom Crean's local airport and, after our submitting two proposals, the board decided against on both occasions.

The second of these proposals was presented, by Eddie, at the 2015 Kerry Airport shareholders AGM in a video compiled painstakingly between myself and another Crean fan, Andy Walsh, whose platform, *Tom Crean Discovery,* is another great online resource helping to increase the number of Crean followers. With a wonderful narration given by Eileen Murphy, the movie still, today, when I watch it, leaves me bursting with pride. Compiled and arranged by novices and featuring a number of high-profile supporters, it left us believing that the great proposal we put forward would at last result in recognition for Crean. Sadly, it didn't.

After the decision of Kerry Airport to decline the opportunity to name the airport in his honour, I decided to rename the platforms. Crean was, after all, an all-Ireland hero; so, in late 2015, the decision was made to alter the name of the Facebook page to *Ireland Should Honour Tom Crean.*

The group was renamed the *Tom Crean Appreciation Society.*

It proved to be a wise decision and the numbers quickly grew as posts that detailed his stories gathered new fans.

There followed an increase in individual tributes from those inspired by Crean's story. Artists were taking to canvasses, singers were writing and performing songs, and others were inspired to pay personal homage to their hero in a variety of crafts.

In 2016, a century after the historic crossing of South Georgia, Tom Crean's granddaughter, Aileen Crean O'Brien, along with her partner and her two sons, set out to re-enact the journey her grandfather made in 1916. They completed the trek but, in the process, Aileen broke her leg after a bad fall and it was, ironically, a Royal Navy ship that came to her rescue to provide her the initial treatment on her road to recovery.

In April 2017, thanks to the idea, the vision and determined efforts of William Kennedy, an engineer with Norwegian Air, brand management within the company were approached to utilise Crean's image on the tail fins of their transatlantic fleet operating from Ireland to the USA. It was a wonderful tribute but still no such recognition has ever been issued to Crean from his own country.

A few months earlier, in December 2016, I created a petition to gather signatures to have an Irish Navy flagship, still in the planning stages, named in honour of Tom Crean and, in little over 12 months, it was signed by over 10,200 people worldwide.

The petition was handed in to the Irish Government Defence Minister on 7th February 2018.

The hope, now, is that Tom Crean's contribution will finally gain official recognition from his country, the one country he loved and had allegiance to, and this is not where his story will end.

In the digital age, his legacy also lives on with devotees who honour him and his achievements across the internet and on social media, and the appetite to learn more about Tom Crean is evident by a growing fan base that, today, stretches across the globe.

No doubt, Tom himself would, were he alive today, shun any notion that he be recognised, such was his character, but Ireland deserves heroes like him every bit as much as he deserves the honour his country should now bestow upon him.

Sketch depictions of two of the most iconic photographs of Tom Crean that were taken by Frank Hurley in 1915 while he was serving on the Endurance expedition.

Today, artists and creators in a variety of genres, who are left inspired by his remarkable story, pay tribute to him in various ways.

TOM CREAN

Dear Sir—I read with deep interest your recent front page story about the coming auction of British Antarctic Expedition letters written by PO Thomas Crean, the Aunascaul explorer, who died in 1938.

I am a life-long student of Crean's leader, Capt. Robert Falcon Scott, as my mother knew Scott, his wife and infant son, now the famous naturalist, Sir Peter Scott.

Crean's career is of epic proportions, and his name should always hold an honoured place not only in Aunascaul but throughout Ireland, undimmed by the passing years.

As a then young journalist, I once heard in an interview from Lt. Edward (Teddy) Evans, later Evans of the Broke, how his life was saved by Crean and Chief Stoker William Lashly, who were both awarded the Albert Medal for their bravery. They, with Scott and four other companion s, were only 59 miles short of the farthest point south every reached by man, when Scott sent Lt. Evans, Crean and Lashly back as the last supporting party. This was before Scott and the four others reached the Pole and died on the return journey.

Evans went down with scurvy, was dragged scores upon scores of miles by Crean and Lashly while strapped face upwards on their sledge until they could go no further. And so Lashly was left with the comatose Evans while Crean marched off on foot in a last ditch rescue attempt. He wsa without a sleeping bag, knowin that he must die if a blizzard came down. Crean had already walked 1,500 miles, hauling a sledge for most of the way, but took with him only a little chocolate and a few biscuits to eat. He reached the Hut Point base in 18 hours — woth one short pause to eat a biscuit — half-an-hour before a blizzard started. He then told a successful rescue party of Evans imploring his companions to leave him in the snow, there to die.

This was the prelude to Crean, who has been described as a giant Irish giant with a profile like that of the Duke of Wellington, buying himself out of the Royal Navy and sacrificing his pension to join the explorer Shackleton in the Endurance. He was one of five who with the leader rowed for 14 days — after the vessel had been crushed by ice — through appalling seas in the ship's boat to South Georgia Island, made famous by the Argentine invasion of the Falklands. With two men, one of them Shackleton, Crean crossed the mountainous island on foot to reach a whaling station and summons aid for the remainder of the Endurance crew stranded on Elephant Island.

Crean's name appeared in the cast on the recent televised *The Last Place on Earth* about Scott and his ill-fated expedition. But I abandoned Scott before my television set long before arrival at the South Pole because many of the characters and the story were twisted so far from the truth that the feelings of condemnation evoked were similar to those felt by a great many others. Scott, who led two Antarctic expeditions, was portrayed as an arrogant, short-sighted ameteur, often at cross swords with his companions, ranged in a first-to-the-Pole contest of Gentlemen against the successful Norwegian professional Players. This is a travesty of the facts.

The expedition, it must be emphasised, achieved tremendously important scientific results. This was led to incalculable benefits in many fields to mankind by research scientists in Antartica down the years.

Yours very sincerely,

DON'T think, however, that these far outposts of pastoral peace are without their romance. As I had swung round the top of Dingle Bay—some days later, admittedly—I spotted in some such forlorn little village the "South Pole Inn." Had it testified of some American place-name of the next parish beyond the Atlantic pond, I would not have been tempted to go in and enquire. But South Pole, I thought, looking at the humped stone bridge over the softly gurgling stream along the heather-clad banks, and at the homely handball alley. Surely!

Yet here lived—and died some years ago—a mile away from his birthplace, Kerryman Tom Crean, from the same village of Annascaul which gave us sculptor Jerome Connor, for ever a name in the chronicles of civilisation. When Robert Falcon Scott asked for volunteers to attempt with him the South Pole, Crean, a farmer's son, one of a family of 14 brothers, "brothers to beat the band," as his bonny, clear-eyed widow put it smilingly—passed the almost super-human tests of the most exacting doctors, combing the fittest out of the thousands of fit, volunteering for this great endeavour.

Poignant Memories

I LOOKED at his portrait in the small, sunny, meticulously clean parlour, a fine, high-browed, strong-jawed, strappingly tall man from Kerry. In the tempest of snow he had set out with his comrades to look for their lost leader. He found him on March 29, 1912, dead, his diary dropped on his chest, his pencil fallen from frozen fingers. I had no eye for the other portraits and mementoes, for the big silver teapot inscribed to "Tom Crean from Ernest and Emily Shackleton," as I thought of standing in the parlour of the man who had found what, to me, had always been one of the most poignant documents in the world's history.

Moving Document

MANY a time I have brought friends in London to see that moving relic, the last pencil scrawls of Scott on his last diary page—written in that last slow day of tortured homeward trek, one long battle with the icy elements—"I do not think I can write more. . . .R Scott." Then, on final impulse: "For God's sake look after our people "

The pencil scrawl slopes down there desperately, like a chart on a seismograph in the worst of an earthquake, to the very bottom of the page. A great man had died, a bold spirit fought to the end, an intrepid sportsman who marched the greatest march ever made, had striven, sought and found—and not yielded.

And here in Kerry lived and died the Irishman who found the mortal remains of that great explorer who *had sought the secrets of the Pole,* to find the secrets of God.

Irish Independent
8th September 1943

197

Tom Crean: One of Kerry's greatest still lacks deserved recognition

TOM CREAN'S episode with the Scott expedition might seem to have been enough adventure for any one man's lifetime, but not for the man from Annascaul. When Ernest Shackleton put together his Antarctic expedition in 1914, shortly before the outbreak of the First World War, Crean was one of the first men chosen and he was appointed second officer. The plan was to traverse the Antarctic from one side to another going via the South Pole.

They never actually set foot on the Antarctic on that expedition because their ship, the Endurance, got stuck in an ice floe. For months they drifted on the floe, hoping that when the southern summer dawned in October 1915 they would break free, but instead their ship began to break up under the pressure of the ice. The Kildare-born Shackleton ordered them to abandon the ship and they decided to make for the nearest land at the uninhabited Elephant Island, some 100 miles away.

The 22 men set out in three boats. Shackleton was in charge of the first, Frank Worsley the second, and Crean the third. It took them six days of sailing and rowing to reach the island. Towards the end of the trip Crean's boat was struggling behind with just three oars, and Worsley dropped back and handed Crean their shortest oar. "Slipper, darlin', what the hell's the good o' givin' me, the longest man, the shortest oar? asked Crean. "Swap it," Worsley shouted and Crean did.

It was some 16 months since they had last set foot on solid ground. They remained on Elephant Island for over four months, sheltering under their upturned boats. But with the southern winter approaching and no sign of help, Shackleton decided that six of them would undertake the perilous 800 mile voyage to South Georgia to get help in the James Caird, the sturdiest of their three small boats.

Historian Ryle Dwyer examines Tom Crean's role in the epic journey of endurance undertaken by Shackleton's team after the failure of their attempt to traverse the Antarctic.

journey across the world's stormiest sea in the small open boat.

Crean acted as cook. Frank Worsley recalled Crean plunging his filthy hands into boiling hooch to remove masses of reindeer hairs that had come off their sleeping bags. Throughout Crean was cheerful and always gang when it was his turn at the tiller. But he was devoid of tune so nobody knew what he was singing, except at more inspirational times when he would burst into 'The Wearing of the Green'.

He got on very well with Shackleton and frequently engaged in mimic bickering in a kind of comic revolt. "Crean's remarks were so Irish," Worsley wrote:

"Go to sleep Crean and don't be clucking like an old hen."

"Boss I can't eat these reindeer hairs. I'll have an inside on me like a billygoat's neck."

"A thousand times it appeared as if the Caird would be engulfed," Shackleton wrote. In the mountainous seas they would at times find themselves suddenly becalmed in a valley of water and then suddenly at the peak of a mountainous swell. They got caught in a hurricane in which a steamer bound for South Georgia actually foundered, but they still managed to reached South Georgia after 16 eventful days. They made land at the uninhabited southern side of the island, which was an adventure in itself because of the sheer, treacherous cliff face.

Another storm struck that night and it was too dangerous to sail around the island, so Shackleton decided that three of them would cross the island on foot. He, Worsley and Crean had to wait nine days for a suitable day and they then set out without overnight provisions. They planned to make the trip to a whaling base at Stormness as fast as possible.

At times they had to climb down almost sheer mountain face lying on their backs and digging foot holds with their heels. They took a chance in using their rope as a sledge by coiling it and the three of them sat on it, locked themselves together and glissaded down a steep slope into the unknown in the clouds below them.

"The speed was terrific. I think we all gasped at that hair-raising shoot into darkness," Worsley wrote. "Then to our joy, the slope curved out, and we shot into a bank of soft snow. We estimated we had shot down a mile in two or three minutes, and had lowered our altitude by two or three thousands feet."

At one point Crean fell through ice and ended up waist deep in a partially frozen lake. After thirty-six hours and covering some 40 miles of mountainous terrain, they finally made Stormness.

They had a pitiable sight, not having washed for months. Their faces and hands were black from

In the early hours of Easter Monday 1916 around the time that Patrick Pearse and company were forming up at Liberty Hall for the Easter Rebellion, the two Irishmen, Crean and Shackleton, set our with four colleagues on their heroic

The James Caird being launched on Elephant Island: what followed became one of the great sea voyages of history.

They loaded the 22-foot boat with supplies after she had been put in the water. "As each boat-load came alongside, the contents were passed to us, with a running fire of jokes, chaff, and good wishes from dear pals whom we were leaving behind," Worsley wrote. "As for Crean, they said things that ought to have made him blush; but what would make Crean blush would make a butcher's dog drop his bone."

Mike Barry in the replica of the 'James Caird' lifeboat, appropriately named the 'Tom Crean' in which an attempt was made this year to retrace the epic sea voyage from Elephant Island to South Georgia. The failure of that attempt underlines the achievement of Crean and the Shackleton team.

> ## In the mountainous seas they would at times find themselves suddenly becalmed in a valley of water and then suddenly at the peak of a mountainous swell.

blubber smoke, their hair and beards matted and their clothes in rags. All three later said that throughout their journey they had felt that there was a fourth person in their party. "Of course," Worsley wrote, "there were only three, but it is strange that in mentally reviewing the crossing we should always think of a fourth, and then correct ourselves."

Next morning the three men went on board a whaler to rescue their three colleagues from the other side of the island and bring them to Stormness and then the following day the three of them set out to rescue the 16 men on Elephant Island. They got to within 60 miles of the island but were forced back by ice and storms.

The Uruguayan government loaned them a trawler that got to within 18 miles of the island, and then Shackleton managed to borrow a small steamer from the Chilean government. In it they finally managed to reach Elephant Island on August 30, 1916, where they found their 16 colleagues living on penguin meat under their upturned boats.

In 1917 Crean married a Corca Dhuibhne girl, Ellen Herlihy. He served out the remainder of the

> ## They were a pitiable sight, not having washed for months. Their faces and hands were black from blubber smoke, their hair and beards matted and their clothes in rags.

Shackleton's ship 'Endurance' trapped in an ice floe before it eventually broke up and sank forcing the team to sail to uninhabited Elephant Island 100 miles away.

Great War in the British Navy and retired to Annascaul in 1920, where he opened a pub, the South Pole Inn. He died on July 27, 1938 and is buried in the graveyard at Ballinacourty, near Annascaul.

Had Tom Crean been of 'the officer class', he would undoubtedly have been celebrated as one of the greatest explorers in history. He deserves to be remembered for his extraordinary heroic feats and his phenomenal endurance which helped to save 23 men in the most trying of circumstances.

Although he was all but forgotten

in this country, he has been celebrated elsewhere. In 1953 Crean Glacier on the island of South Georgia was named in his honour, and in 1985 the Australians named Mount Crean in the mountains that he had crossed when going for help for his colleagues in 1912. Surely it is time that a suitable section of Kerry County Museum was set aside to commemorate his extraordinary feats.

The two faces of Antarctic explorer Tom Crean from Annascaul.

LEFT: The rugged Irish man whom Scott noted was 'ready to do anything and go anywhere, the harder the work, the better.'

RIGHT: Tom Crean as a petty officer on the Royal Navy: 'an excellent man, tall with a profile like the Duke of Wellington, universally liked.'

Shackleton's ship 'Endurance' sets out from Millwall Docks, London on August 1, 1914, with Tom Crean at the helm.

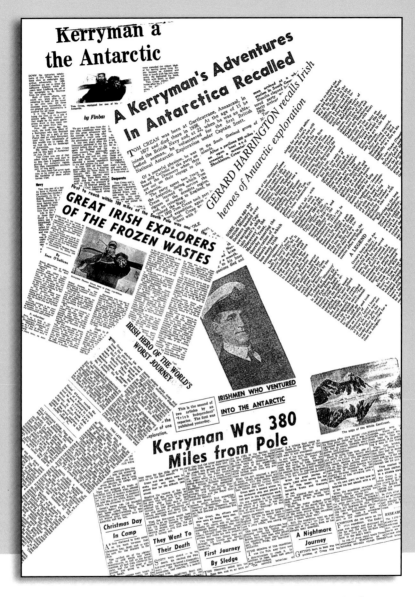

News articles that highlighted Crean's story in the 20th Century

Irish Independent 30th December 1955 (Kerryman was 380 miles from the Pole)
Connaught Tribune 3rd August 1957 (Irish Hero of the World's Worst Journey)
Irish Press 1st January 1958 (Great Irish Explorers of the Frozen Wastes)
Kerryman 11th January 1958 (A Kerryman's Adventures in Antarctica Recalled)
Kerryman 15th July 1977 (Kerryman at the Antarctic)
Southern Star 8th December 1996 (Heroes of Antarctic Exploration)

MAKING HISTORY IN THE KINGDOM

A hero for all seasons

Tom Crean's *Endurance* epic began 100 years ago this month

Tom and Ellen Crean with their daughters Mary and Eileen in the 1920s.

A hundred years ago this month, Tom Crean was on board the *Endurance* when it became trapped in ice on the way to the South Pole. RYLE DWYER says that if the Annascaul man had been of the 'officer class' he would have been celebrated as one of the greatest explorers in history.

RYLE DWYER

FOR A COMBINATION of courage and endurance, the feats of Tom Crean from Annascaul were truly outstanding. Had Tom Crean been of the 'officer class', he would undoubtedly have been celebrated as one of the greatest explorers in history.

He deserves to be remembered for his extraordinary heroic feats and his phenomenal endurance, which helped to save so many men in the most trying of circumstances.

Around this time one hundred years ago - in January 1915 - he was part of the expedition led by Kildare-born Ernest Shackleton aiming to become the first people to cross the Antarctic from one side to the other via the South Pole.

They had set out from Britain just before the outbreak of the first World War, and the rest of the world promptly lost interest in the midst of the carnage and turmoil of the so-called Great War.

They were essentially forgotten whilst engaged in one of the greatest adventures of all time.

Their ship, *Endurance*, got caught in an ice floe in January 1915, and they drifted for the next eight months before the ship got crushed in the ice.

None of the 28-men ever actually set foot on the Antarctic during the expedition. They managed to salvage three lifeboats, and Shackleton decided to head for uninhabited Elephant Island, a hundred miles away.

They set out in the three boats, with Shackleton in charge of one. Frank Worsley, the captain of the *Endurance*, took charge of a second, while Crean led the third.

It took six days sailing and rowing to reach Elephant Island. It was some sixteen months since they had last set foot on solid ground. They remained on Elephant Island for over four months, sheltering under their upturned boats, and eating penguin meat.

With the southern winter approaching and no sign of help, Shackleton decided that six of them would take the perilous 900-mile journey to the island of South Georgia for help in the *James Caird*. Although slightly under 22.5 feet in length, it was their sturdiest boat. Shackleton's first choices to make the journey were Worsley and Crean.

Worsley was chosen for his navigational skills, while Crean was obviously selected for his experience and the extraordinary prowess he had already demonstrated in tight situations on earlier Antarctic expeditions.

In the early hours of Easter Monday 1916 -

around the time that Patrick Pearse and company were forming up at Liberty Hall for the Easter Rebellion - the two Irishmen, Crean and Shackleton, set out with four colleagues on their heroic journey across the stormy ocean in a small boat.

Crean acted as cook. Frank Worsley recalled Crean plunging his filthy hands into boiling hooch to remove masses of reindeer hairs that had come off their sleeping bags.

Throughout, Crean was cheerful and always sang during his turn at the tiller, but he was tone deaf, so nobody knew what he was singing, except at more inspirational moments when he would burst into 'The Wearing of the Green'.

He got on very well with Shackleton and frequently engaged in mimic bickering in a kind of comic revolt.

"Crean's remarks were so Irish," Worsley wrote. 'Go to sleep and don't be clucking like an old hen' and 'Boss I can't eat these reindeer hairs. I'll have an inside on me like a billygoat's neck'."

They got caught in a hurricane in which a steamer bound for South Georgia actually foundered.

STORM

"A thousand times it appeared as if the *Caird* would be engulfed," Shackleton wrote. At one moment they would find themselves suddenly becalmed in a valley of water and then just as quickly at the peak of a mountainous swell.

After 17 eventful days they made land at the uninhabited southern side of South Georgia. Their boat's rudder broke off during the landing.

Another storm struck that night. Shackleton decided that three of them would cross the island on foot, but he, Worsley and Crean had to wait nine days for a suitable day.

They then set out without overnight provisions. They planned to make the trip to the whaling base at Stromness as fast as possible. They had to descend at almost sheer mountain face lying on their back and digging footholds with their heels. At another point they coiled the rope and locked themselves together, using the coiled rope as a sledge.

They proceeded to slide down a steep slope

into the unknown in the clouds below them. "The speed was terrific. I think we all gasped at that hair-raising shoot into darkness," Worsley wrote.

"Then, to our joy, the slope curved out, and we shot into a bank of soft snow. We estimated we had shot down a mile in two or three minutes, and had lowered our altitude by two or three thousand feet."

At one point, Crean fell through ice and ended up waist deep in a partially frozen lake. After covering some forty miles of mountainous terrain in thirty-six hours, they finally reached the whaling station at Stromness.

They were a pitiable sight, not having washed for months.

Their faces and hands were black from blubber smoke, their hair and beards matted and their clothes in rags.

Next morning, the three men went on board a whaler to rescue their three colleagues on the other side of the island.

The day after that, the three of them set out to rescue their 22 colleagues on Elephant Island.

They got to within 60 miles of the island but were forced back by ice and storms.

The Uruguayan government loaned them a trawler that got to within eighteen miles of the island, and then Shackleton managed to borrow a small steamer from the Chilean government.

In it, they finally managed to reach Elephant Island on August 30th, 1916, where they found their colleagues still living on penguin meat under their upturned boats.

No longer the forgotten man

Born at Gurtuchrane near Annascaul on August 20th, 1877, Tom Crean had run away from home to join the Royal Navy as a fifteen-year-old. He was part of Robert Scott's 1901-04 expedition to the Antarctic, and he later distinguished himself in Scott's second expedition, which was part of the epic race to become the first humans to reach the South Pole.

In 1917, Crean married a Corcaduibhne girl, Ellen Herlihy. He survived the first World War in the British Navy and retired to Annascaul in 1920, where he opened a pub, the South Pole Inn.

He died on July 27th, 1938, and is buried in the graveyard at Ballinacourty, near Annascaul.

While he was all but forgotten in this country until the late 1990s, Tom Crean has been celebrated elsewhere. In 1953, a glacier on the island of South Georgia was named after him, and in 1965 the Australians named the Antarctic mountain that he had crossed in going for help for his colleagues in 1912 Mount Crean.

It has only been in the last twenty years, however, that Crean's story has received anything like the publicity it deserved in this country.

ACHIEVEMENT

In January 1997 an Irish group sought to emulate the voyage from Elephant Island to South Georgia in a 23-foot boat, aptly name *The Tom Crean*.

They had the advantage of a sturdy escort vessel shadowing them in case of emergency.

Even though it was the height of the South Atlantic summer, *The Tom Crean* got caught in two Force 10 storms during which it rolled three times. The crew decided to abandon the venture on learning of the approach of another storm.

Against their failure, the achievement of Shackleton and his colleagues stood out all the more.

Crean's story was further boosted by the publication in 2000 of Michael Smith's highly acclaimed biography, *An Unsung Hero: Tom Crean - Antarctic Survivor*.

The following year TG4 produced a documentary on the exploits of Crean under the title *Ciarraíoch san Oighir (A Kerryman in the Ice)*.

A bronze sculpture of Crean was unveiled in Annascaul by his daughters Mary O'Brien and the late Eileen O'Brien in July 2003, and Guinness began using the name and image of Tom Crean in its advertising the following month.

The same year *Tom Crean: Antarctic Explorer*, a one-man play written and performed by Aidan Dooley, premiered in New York and then toured around the world.

In 2011 Charlie Bird featured in a RTE documentary, *On the Trail of Tom Crean*. Why was he forgotten in this country for so long?

The petition being handed over to Paul Kehoe TD, Irish Minister for Defence, in February 2018 by Eileen Percival, landlady of the South Pole Inn and Dublin schoolgirl, Lea Carey

EPILOGUE

I wrote this book with a clear motive - to help bring attention to the story of Tom Crean. I hope it also wins new fans to the case for national recognition in his home country.

It would be impossible to write a book about Crean without referencing his life before and after Antarctica.

I have never set foot on anything colder than an icy Manchester pavement - so, I value greatly the accounts of those explorers who were there or who have been there since. Reading and hearing their documented experiences was the only way I could have attempted to interpret what it was like for Crean to confront, and navigate across, Antartica's harsh environment.

The burning question I was left with after researching and writing this book was: what was it about the most inhospitable place on the planet, that made men like Crean, Shackleton, Scott, Lashly, Amundsen, Worsley, Wild and others want to keep returning there? Could it be that there was a handful of men who returned for the excitement of it? Was it, perhaps, for the comradeship?

Of course, at the turn of the last century, discovery was a major factor, as was the kudos and glory for some, but I believe there are also less obvious factors at play.

One of the books that I've acknowledged is 'Of Whales And Men' by R. B. Robertson, a ship doctor's account of the dying whaling industry in the Southern Ocean. Within its passages, I believe I may have found some of the explanations to that burning question.

One of the characters in Robertson's book goes on to state:

"The relationships and bonds formed on the expeditions were second only to a love relationship. It's a relationship that can be found in war but, in Antarctica, it's not man against man, it's man backed by his comrades against the worst that the elements of nature can throw at them."

Maybe it was also the urge to see what was over the next hill when Antarctica was one of the only places in the world where it was still possible to look over a hill without knowing for certain what you might see. It could be more snow, more ice, but it might not be - and it's that 'might' that brought them back time and again.

Perhaps some who returned did so because they felt more at home there than they did in the societies they'd left behind.

After his first expedition, Tom Crean returned twice more and, in his own words, he *"looked forward"* to a fourth expedition; that phrase alone tells us of his desire to return but it does not offer his reasons.

My belief is that he wanted to return because it was the place he found his true calling. He earned the respect of colleagues who placed great value on his abilities and, of course, people are drawn to those opportunities that allow them to demonstrate their best skills.

Whatever the reasons, many descendants of his comrades are thankful that he did return. For the men of this era who spent much of their careers in Antarctica, it's a question we'll have to continue to speculate about.

Researching for the book also took me on an expedition of my own and it's one that's led me to a deeper admiration for the exploits of the crews who pioneered polar exploration. The gallantry, bravery, the physical and mental suffering of the men mentioned in this book are astonishing. Aside from my long-held admiration for Tom Crean, I have discovered a renewed respect for one man in particular - Sir Ernest Shackleton.

What drove Shackleton to seek world firsts on the most difficult path a person could opt for is open to question. I'm sure far easier avenues of exploration could have been sought if it were just for the honours and popularity that followed.

What my research did reveal was that Shackleton was a man with an obsession for adventure and, if he were alive today, I'm sure he would seek out the undiscovered and head straight there by hook or by crook. The greater the challenge, the greater the attraction.

What made him a respected leader was his desire to share that glory and he did this with a trusted nucleus of companions who became his friends. Every man who served under Shackleton's leadership respected him, even those he had cause to discipline. Their term for him - 'The Boss' - was borne out of solid affection. When the chips were down, he was relentless in raising the spirits of his men and when all seemed lost, he found a way out. Shackleton's sense of responsibility to those serving under him superseded any sense of danger to himself. It's a rare trait that truly defines greatness.

Commenting on his loss to a Daily Mail reporter on 30th January 1922, his friend John Rowlett answered in a most fitting tribute to the great man:

"What can I say? Ernest Shackleton was my best friend. I have known him almost all my life, since the time when we were boys together at Dulwich College. I shall count it the greatest privilege of my career to have been associated with him in what has tragically proved to be his last expedition. His one thought was

to help science, regardless of self and to uphold the honour of British exploration. Everyone who came into contact with him realised that his was a great personality. He was such a generous soul - idealistic, impulsive and ready to help anybody in trouble."

In the course of my research, I came across the story of another man who had considered Tom Crean a hero yet, by his own actions, as the *Lusitania* sank, proved to be a hero himself. The name of Joseph Foster Stackhouse can never be ranked alongside those of Shackleton or Scott in the realms of polar exploration but he stands shoulder to shoulder with any of the great heroes of the time who were prepared to lay down their lives to save others. Discovering his story and the connection to Tom Crean is something I'm delighted to have included in this book.

It was also while researching those associated with Tom Crean, that I happened upon two other Kerrymen from the same humble beginnings who also acquitted themselves highly in the course of their careers.

Daniel O'Sullivan, the Tralee born native who was among the first to greet Crean, Shackleton and Worsley when they returned to Port Stanley after the first failed rescue attempt aboard the whaler, *Southern Sky*, had risen through the ranks to become the Chief Constable of the Falkland Islands Police Force.

Born in Blennerville, County Kerry, in February 1876, Daniel, a young fisherman, took the same route as Crean by joining the Royal Navy. Like Crean, he served on both *HMS Cambridge* and *HMS Defiance* at Devonport and the two men very likely became acquainted at this time.

In 1898 Daniel was assigned to *HMS Flora* sailing out of

Devonport for the south-east coast of America. In 1900 he left *Flora* for the Admiralty Coaling Station in the Falkland Islands. Having served seven of his twelve year tenure in the Royal Navy, Daniel, evidently attracted by what the island had to offer him, purchased his way out of the navy for the sum of £12 in 1901 (approximately £1450 in todays currency) by which time he'd reached the rating of Petty Officer 2nd Class.[1]

While in the Falklands, Daniel came to the rescue of an Italian man who fell from a small boat into the water while returning from Port Stanley to the coaling station.

Daniel, who witnessed the fall, jumped in still fully clothed and recovered the man who was lying on his back on the harbour bottom.[2]

Daniel was not the only bravehearted compatriot of Crean to distinguish himself while serving in the Royal Navy. Born in Minard in April 1877, just two months later than Tom Crean, Patrick Brosnan also began his Naval career aboard *HMS Impregnable* in 1893 and, like Crean, he too will have suffered from the harsh regime that young boys were subjected to at the time. However, Patrick rose steadily through the ranks reaching the status of Chief Petty Officer before his retirement in 1918, also earning the esteemed accolade of being 'mentioned in despatches.' Although I was unable to determine the details, what is certain is that only acts of bravery were rewarded with such an honour.[3]

Perhaps it was the times that produced such men of mettle; they were determined to establish themselves in order to change their fortunes. Whatever it was, there was certainly no shortage of personal bravery in this group of Irishmen - who all displayed the qualities described by Foster Stackhouse as being those that made for the best explorers.

On the subject of Crean connections, I'm proud to have become a member of the 'I may be related to Tom Crean' club that grows as people discover more about him.

In February 1896 at the Catholic church in Annascaul, my grandfather, Timothy D. Foley, married a local woman, Hanoria Courtney from the nearby townland of Coumduff.

Courtney also happened to be the maiden name of Tom Crean's mother, Catherine.

Ironically, I only discovered this four years after I had created the social media campaign to honour Tom Crean and it's possible that I can claim some possible family connection, albeit a tenuous one, given that Hanoria was my grandfather's first wife and was not my grandmother. Nevertheless, the family link to Annascaul continues to this day and my father's sister married and raised a family who still reside there.

As a young man in the 1930s, my father, also Tim Foley, travelled daily the 13 miles from his home in Shanahill, Keel, to work in Annascaul.

For a while, he worked with his sister at the local dentist, Patrick J. O'Neill's, house at nearby Bunaneer. It was a place Crean often frequented when walking his dogs and the dentist, a former Captain of the Kerry Brigade in the pre-treaty days who had been sentenced to five years internment in 1921, was well acquainted with Tom Crean who he served alongside on the Annascaul Coal Committee.

On 10th April 1935, Patrick J O'Neill died suddenly. After a funeral mass at Annascaul church with his coffin draped in the tricolour, his former comrades carried the coffin to Inch graveyard. His funeral was attended by Tom Crean and perhaps it was a time that both of my heroes, my father and Tom Crean, were present at the same location on the same day.[4]

While in Annascaul, my father would often stay at his sister's house in Ballintaggart and his only recollections of the man he often passed, but who he knew had served with Captain Scott, were that he was referred to by villagers as 'Tom the Pole.' During Crean's lifetime, my father and many others in the locality knew little else about the legend in their midst.

Much of my life meant long holidays spent in my father's birthplace in Keel, County Kerry, and, throughout most of that time, I've known of and have been a huge admirer of Tom Crean. The journey I have been on while writing this book uncovered new information about Tom Crean and this served to strengthen a resolve to see him honoured by his country.

Today, a growing band of supporters from all over the world are adding their names to the call for Ireland to provide him the official recognition he richly deserves.

If, after reading about his exploits and about this great man, you'd like to play a part, then you'd be most welcome to join us. Signing the petition and liking our social media platforms will help grow our numbers and assist in bringing about official recognition for a remarkable man.

I hope the stories of my hero inspire you as much as they have me.

APPENDIX

A COMPILATION OF RELATED MATTER

Tom Crean Letter - Scott's Final Journey

In a letter sent to his friend, Captain R. H. Dodds, circa 1918,[1] Tom Crean outlined the reasons for the demise of Scott and the polar party on their return trip after losing the race to the pole.

'Scott's Last Antarctic Expedition.'

"Left Cardiff, June 1910. Arrived New Zealand, November 1910. Left New Zealand, December 1910. Arrived in ice, January 23rd 1911. Left Hut Point on long march, November 1st 1911 to December 6th 1911, when we parted sleeping accommodation but remained in company until January 4th 1912. On this date, there not being enough food, Lashly, Lieut. Evans and myself had to turn back to allow the others more supplies. January 4th was last I saw of Captain Oates, on which date I left his party 130 miles from the South Pole. Captain Scott, Captain Oates, Dr Wilson, Lieut. Bowers and Petty Officer Evans went on from now and all reached the South Pole on January 17th, 1912. On their return, however, owing to lack of food, the party gradually dwindled. 310 miles from home, Evans went, 174, Captain Oates died (on March 17th 1912) while Captain Scott, Dr Wilson and Lieut. Bowers perished 150 miles from home on March 29th 1912. They perished owing entirely to lack of food, which was mainly caused through stress of weather holding them many days on short

rations and, when the party should have marched nine miles a day from food depot to food depot, they were only able to do six and gradually dwindled to even less; thus, not reaching the depots in question. It is actually proved that Scott, Wilson and Bowers lived for nine days on two days' rations... I was one of the search party to look for their last resting place and was first of the search party to see it some 14 miles away from One Ton Camp on November 15th 1912. I noticed what appeared to be a flagstaff about 400 yards on my right. When I entered, I found Wilson and Bowers were tied up in their bags but poor Scott was not, proving that he died last and had been able to fasten up the bags of the others. They had all died as proper English gentlemen, although they were given the necessary medicine to take their own lives, if they so desired... I have now fulfilled three expeditions but will look forward to a fourth."

It is clear from the content that, although the group were chronically short of food, it was worsening weather conditions that prevented further progress.

No one had expected a tragic outcome for Scott and his party and, soon after the fate of the polar party was announced following the return of *Terra Nova* in February 1913, there was a media scramble to cover the story and to determine the cause. It remains a story that generates speculation and conjecture to this day, with one recent account even suggesting that skullduggery may have played a part. It is a ridiculous notion to entertain thoughts of deliberate sabotage causing the demise of Scott and his colleagues in a place where men relied entirely on the honour and brotherhood of one another.

With hindsight, every fatality can be reassessed as a means of determining how it could have been prevented and surviving expedition members will have mulled this over in the aftermath of the tragedy.

Antarctica was a place where risks to life were great and Scott and his party were fully accepting of the dangers on their last, fateful journey.

One correspondent recalled an interview he had with Scott before he sailed out on the expedition from London.[2] Eager for a quote for publication, he asked:

"What if you don't come back?"

In reply, Scott said, *"Well, if I don't come back, you may rely upon it that I'm dead and when you know I'm dead I'll let you say this."*

At this, the correspondent transcribed Scott's words in shorthand in a note he would treasure as a souvenir:

"It is my intention to find the South Pole. If I fail the first time, I shall know why I fail and try again. It is my desire to keep trying until I succeed. No effort of which I am capable will be spared. So far as human ingenuity and our means can devise, we shall eliminate danger but there will be a risk, possibly a great risk, and that risk we are prepared to face cheerfully. If I never return, England will know that I and those with me have done our best and will give us credit for our work."

It's a poignant reminder of Scott's thoughts before he set out on what was to be his last expedition. He, and the men who served under him, did indeed do their best.

Tom Crean and the Polar Party - What If?

What would have happened had Tom Crean been one of the party chosen to go to the South Pole with Captain Scott?

It's the burning question that most admirers of Tom Crean have an opinion on and of course it is one that cannot be definitively answered, but it can be explored.

I consider that it would have been expected for Crean to be a member of the final group that headed to the South Pole if we account for his time in service with Scott after the *Discovery* expedition

On 18th September 1906, when Tom Crean joined the crew of *HMS Victorious* between further attachments to the shore-based barracks *HMS Pembroke* at Chatham, it was the first of four postings alongside Scott: on *HMS Albemarle* (1907), *HMS Essex* (1908), and *HMS Bulwark* (1909).

That Scott specifically chose Crean to serve as his coxswain in the period leading up to the *Terra Nova* expedition is reason enough to believe that he would be in Scott's final party but he wasn't so why was this?

To understand this better other avenues have to be explored for possible answers.

Up to the point of Scott's decision on 4th January 1912, two of the eight men present on the Polar plateau, Lieutenant Teddy Evans, Scott's second in command, and William Lashly, had trudged their way to the Pole a week before the final parties set out on 1st November 1911.

Both men were spent and Scott, being aware of this, ruled them out as candidates. It was a surprise that Scott decided on a final party of five and before *Terra Nova* left New Zealand in November 1910, he laid out his plans quite clearly stating:

"The main travelling party for the Pole will consist of sixteen men. After a certain distance has been traversed, four will go back and the remainder will continue the journey. Subsequently, another four will return to our base and after one more stage has been covered a third quartet will turn around and retrace their steps northward, leaving four men to continue the last stage of the journey. No decision as to who will make up the last party of four will be arrived at until the last moment, that depending upon the physical condition of the men at the time. Obviously, the fittest persons will be selected."3

What we can determine from this is that Scott appeared to make his unconventional choice sometime later. Exactly when has been the subject of speculation ever since and theories are abound that he may have discussed his intentions with Wilson long before reaching the Polar plateau. Others link Scott's intentions with the moving film sequences of a camp drill taken by Ponting back at Cape Evans. In it, Scott along with Wilson, Edgar Evans and Bowers were featured in the primary roles. Oates, it has been assumed, was chosen because he was the army's sole representative and because he'd contributed financially to the expedition.

Scott had in part, kept his word in choosing the fittest persons to accompany him but, as already referred to in a previous chapter, he had to make use of a concocted blag to render Tom Crean unfit to make the journey with him.

He and the polar party now faced a 150-mile trek to the Pole with a return journey of almost 900 miles. The lower decks representative on the journey would be Edgar Evans, not Tom Crean.

Edgar first met Scott when he was assigned to *HMS Majestic* in 1899 while Scott was serving as the ship's torpedo Lieutenant. It was while serving on *Majestic* that Scott first heard about the proposed expedition to Antarctica and within two days he applied to lead it. It is very possible that Edgar volunteered his services on the *Discovery* expedition to his Commander at this time.

Twelve years later and just days before heading off to the South Pole, Scott wrote to Edgar Evans's wife. The letter provides us with an insight into the close relationship he had with the Welshman. In it he wrote:

> *"Although I have never met you, your husband has told me a great deal about you so that I can imagine that you and the children will be waiting to see him home again next year....he is very well indeed, very strong and in very good condition.*
>
> *It is possible we may not finish our work this year and in that case he will stop with me for a second season. If so you must try and remember that he is certain to be in the best of health and that it will be all the better when he does come home.*
>
> *When that time comes I hope he will get some good billet and not have to leave you again. He is such an old friend of mine and has done so well on this Expedition that he deserves all I can do for him. So I must hope you won't be anxious or worried."[4]*

In the years after the *Discovery* expedition before *Terra Nova* set sail in 1910, both Scott and Evans had married, (Edgar in 1904 and Scott in 1908) and both were fathers. It was a shared connection that may have elevated their relationship to such a level that allowed Scott the comfort of corresponding so warmly with Evans' wife.

It is possible that Scott's decision to take Edgar was one made as much from the heart as the head. Certainly, Scott's letter to Edgar's wife Lois, suggests he had earmarked her husband as a member of the final group.

Tom Crean, at the time of his being chosen for the *Terra Nova* expedition, was still a bachelor and it had been entirely through good fortune that he had been recruited to join the pioneering Discovery expedition in 1901.

For Scott, the decision may have been a difficult one but a longer association and closer ties to Evans could well have been the deal breaker. The role that the class-system played in Scott making his decision would prevent any notion of taking two men from the lower decks, (ratings), on the trail to glory, so having two of his favoured sledgers on the trek to the Pole would have been out of the question.

Evans had sustained a cut to his hand on the party's approach to the South Pole and it was an injury that never healed. Its debilitating effects could have been the cause of his delaying the party on their return trip as his condition worsened. He then suffered a fall into a crevasse causing a head injury which further slowed him down and led to his ultimate demise.

Under Antarctic conditions, minor cuts can morph into a more serious injury that could prove fatal, as they did with Edgar Evans on 17th February 1912. Had he not become a victim to injury, Evans would comfortably have kept pace with his colleagues. Being the largest of the party, Evans required a greater calorie intake than his colleagues and this, combined with his two injuries, provides us with the reasons why he was the first of the party to fall victim.

Consequently, the delays caused by Evans's injuries lessened the food rations for the remaining members and affected their ability to continue on a schedule that would have allowed them to reach food depots on time. Added to this were the adverse weather conditions that confined the party to their tent. Stepping outside into the severe blizzards meant certain death and it's a sacrifice Captain Oates made when leaving the tent on 16th March 1912.

Just 11 miles short of *One Ton Depot*, which, had they reached, would have seen their chances of survival improve dramatically, the remaining members of the Polar party became prisoners to the weather. Dwindling food and fuel supplies lessened their chances of survival.

The continuing blizzards led them to accept their fate and it's the story that overshadowed the tale of survival of the last supporting party of Tom Crean, William Lashly and Edward Evans. Of course, it's entirely understandable that the story of the Polar party's demise would populate the world's press and Tom Crean's epic solo march was a forgotten footnote that became legend only among the Polar fraternity in the aftermath of the tragedy.

And so to the question: What if Tom Crean had been chosen as one of the group who accompanied Scott to the pole?

Opinions on the matter have to be based entirely on supposition and mine is no different.

As he was, at the time of parting from the Polar group, injury-free, Tom Crean would, I believe, if chosen by Scott, have escorted the return party to *One Ton Depot* - but only if weather conditions allowed and that he remained free from injury.

Writing in 1919, about his analysis of weather conditions, George Simpson, the expedition's meteorologist, stated it, "'*probable that 1912 was an abnormal year"* and that his own findings offered, *"further support for the contention that Captain Scott experienced unusually low temperatures on his return from the Pole."*[5]

Modern scientific methods comparing temperatures recorded by the polar party along the route of their final steps with those taken since 1985, appear to have established that the harsh temperatures Scott and his companions recorded in 1912 were freakish and were a major contributing factor to their demise.[6] However, a more recent study, the findings of which were included in a controversial book, disputes the conclusions of the previous study and had the luxury of an additional 10 years of Antarctic weather analysis.[7]

The events that took place in 1912, over the first three months of the *Terra Nova* expedition have generated conflicting views on the possible causes of the tragedy ever since. The debate on whether Tom Crean's inclusion in the polar party would have made any difference, is one that presents a possible prevention but like every other theory, it is based upon supposition and conjecture.

If we assume that the weather was abnormally severe and would still have hampered their progress had Crean been among the final five, would his presence have made a difference?

It is another impossible question to answer. As we don't have a window to the past, we don't know if any breaks in the weather would have allowed them to make it to *One Ton Depot* on schedule. I'm certain their chances of doing so would have improved with an injury-free Tom Crean in tow but without conclusive weather data we can only base our opinions on hypotheses.

Those of us enamoured by Tom Crean's story, consider him al-most superhuman and we can become guilty of being a little over-ex-pectant in his abilities. Tom Crean was undoubtedly a man capable of incredible feats of endurance in extreme conditions but he too would have perished under the same weather conditions and lack of provisions that sealed the fate of the polar party in March 1912.

Conversely, had Edgar Evans been returned back to base - what would have become of the return party?

Lieutenant Teddy Evans would still have suffered with scurvy and Edgar Evans's hand injury would have worsened making it an almost impossible task for William Lashly to shoulder the responsibility of caring for two sick men.

The theories here are populated with so many 'ifs' and so many possible outcomes. There is a case for and against all arguments based on various scenarios but nothing will ever prove conclusive. However, it won't stop Tom Crean admirers from across the world voicing their opinion on the matter.

So, having started this discussion with one question, it can only be concluded with many more.

Tributes In Honour Of Tom Crean

In Ireland, one solitary, privately funded statue to commemorate Tom Crean stands across the road from his former home, the *South Pole Inn*. The Tom Crean memorial garden and the bronze sculpture, depicting Tom holding the puppies he was so fond of, is a place of pilgrimage for his many admirers across the world.

His memory is served across the world by the following natural features:

- *Crean Glacier - a four-mile-long ice sheet on the north coast of South Georgia.*
- *Mount Crean - an 8,630ft peak in South Victoria Land, Antarctica.*
- *Crean Lake - a Lake on the island of South Georgia.*
- *Crean Deep - a 29km x 9km feature off the coast of New Zealand that forms part of one of Earth's deepest underwater trenches.*
- *Mount Crean - another mountain named in Crean's honour. The small peak of 2,300ft lies in Eastern Greenland.*
- *Crean 01400 - meteorites discovered on Mount Crean by a team of geologists in 2001.*

Tom's Parents, Brothers and Sisters: My findings

I really do not envy anyone tasked with researching countless collections to discover the ancestry of their own or others' families. However, it is, without doubt, thrilling to uncover some hitherto unknown facts.

It came as no surprise in my research to find that many people searching for their Annascaul roots, who've become aware of the man and his story, have a particular outcome in mind - *"Am I related to Tom Crean?"*

Many are convinced they are but determining this is difficult because the names Crean and Courtney/Cournane are very popular surnames, particularly on the Dingle peninsula.

And, so, to my findings:

Church records differ from Civic records and event dates rarely marry up. Civic records that register the birth certificate are documented later than when the birth actually took place. The best barometer of the actual date of a child's birth can be found in the ledgers kept by the parish priest, many of which are documented in the Catholic Parish Registers at the National Library of Ireland. A problem arises when the parish records are missing or difficult to locate; many were - including most of Tom Crean's siblings and his parents.

The Civic records, however, contained the birth documents of Tom Crean and all of his siblings bar his eldest brother, Hugh, whose details happened to still remain in the parish register where his name was listed as 'Hugo.'

Soon after a birth, and, in some cases, on the same day, newborns in 19th century Ireland were baptised. One particular entry led me to an absolute belief that Tom Crean was born over week earlier than we assumed.

In the diocese of County Kerry, the parish of Ballanvohir encompasses the area in and around Annascaul. Registered as 'Joanna' Crean, a child was born to Patrick Crean and Catherine Crean (née Cournane) of Gortacurraun on 16th February 1877. This birth, I believe to be that of Tom Crean and that the name error could be put down to any number of factors. Parish ledgers were not drawn up immediately after an event took place and it is entirely plausible that a priest, having undertaken many baptisms, marriages and funerals in the time before compiling the register, made a mistake. Quite apart from this, the parish register records the birth nine days before 25th February date written on the birth certificate of Tom Crean that was registered in Dingle on 11th March 1877. There is no doubt in my mind that 'Joanna' and 'Thomas' are one and the same person. It is somewhat paradoxical that a man such as Tom Crean should enter the world recorded under a female name but no other logical explanation can be concluded from existing records.

So, given that we have no definitive proof as to whether the child was baptised on the same day as the birth, I believe Tom Crean's official birthdate should now be rewritten as 16th February 1877.

In the table following are the rest of my findings and I'm still left a little disappointed that I could not determine more details about two of Tom's brothers, Patrick and John.

After scouring through passenger lists I discovered that Crean's two younger brothers emigrated - Michael to Boston in the USA in 1901 and Martin to Quebec in Canada in 1912. As to their whereabouts thereafter the trail ran dry.

Not being privy to the information that any of the direct descendants may already have, it would be interesting to learn more about John and Patrick. I was unable to find any of their details beyond their birth dates. In the 1911 Census, details for Catherine Crean state that she had given birth to eleven children of which eight were still alive. We know that, by this time, her eldest son, Hugh, had passed away in 1908; so, two of three brothers we cannot account for in the 1911 census had also died before these Census details were recorded. That equates to two of either John, Patrick or Michael having also passed away by 1911.

On the matter of Tom Crean's parents, we can fairly determine

Catherine's date of birth to 1839 based on her death certificate. One baptism entry did catch my eye - that of Catherine Cournane born to Cornelius Cournane and Mary Flaherty of Castlegreory on 18th December 1839 but I could find no definitive proof that she was Tom Crean's mother.

As for Patrick, Tom's father, the loss of any parent is a significant event in anyone's life and I would like to have documented his passing in the book but I found nothing in my search.

It's clear that Patrick passed away after the marriage of Tom Crean in 1917 and before the death of his wife Catherine in 1924, and evidence of this can be found in the marriage announcement and on Catherine's death certificate which recorded her as being a widow.

Generally, when a marriage was reported, the details would indicate whether a parent of the bride or groom had passed away by stating, for example: 'Thomas Crean, son of Mrs Catherine Crean and the late Mr Patrick Crean." In the absence of such as statement on Tom Crean's marriage certificate, this suggests that Patrick was still alive in 1917.

As you can imagine, record-keeping of the time was not always to the letter. We also know that some records were lost; so, maybe we are destined never to learn more. Or perhaps someone out there already does?

Children of Patrick and Catherine Crean
(Based on information sourced via Church and Civil Records)

Patrick Crean
No definitive birthdate. Unable to determine a date of death. Died after 1917 and prior to the death of his wife in 1924

Catherine Crean née Courtney
No definitive birthdate found. Died 15th September 1924 at Gortacarraun

Name	Birth Certificate and/or Baptism Entry	Notes
Hugh	Baptised on 7th November 1867	Married Johanna Connor, in Annascaul, 18th February 1896. Died 24th March 1908
Mary	11th March 1869	No marriage record discovered and unable to determine date of death. In the 1901 Census Mary is listed working as a servant at the home of Maurice Fitzgerald of Drom West, Cloghane, County Kerry. Appeared on 1911 census aged 42 still residing with parents at Gortacurraun.
John	13th June 1870	Not listed in 1901 or 1911 Census for returns at Gortacurraun. Unable to determine date of death.
Cornelius	2nd October 1871	Became a Constable in RIC and married Annie Stanton of Cork at St Patrick's Church, Cork, 11th September 1906. Shot dead in ambush on 25th April 1920.

Name	Birth Certificate and/or Baptism Entry	Notes
Daniel	15th April 1873	Married Margaret Curran of Minard East, 13th February 1912. Died 3rd June 1932 at Gortacurraun.
Patrick	24th March 1875	Not listed on 1901 or 1911 Census for returns at Gortacurraun. Unable to determine date of death.
Thomas	25th February 1877/Baptised 16th February 1877	Married Ellen Herlihy at Annascaul on 5th September 1917. Died 27th July 1938.
Michael	14th March 1879	Detailed as living at Gortacurraun with parents aged 22 in 1901 Census. Emigrated to Boston, USA on board *SS Commonwealth* later in 1901
Johanna	4th April 1881	Married Thomas Devane of Glenminard at Annascaul on 22nd February, 1908. Unable to determine date of death
Martin	15th March 1883	Detailed as living at Gortacurraun with his parents aged 26 in 1911 Census. Emigrated to Quebec, Canada on board *RMS Virginian* in 1912
Catherine	23rd August 1887	Married Constable Daniel Donovan of Annascaul on 21st September 1915 at Annascaul

Meeting Tom Crean's eldest daughter, Mary, in 2011 was a great honour for me. Mary was a wonderful woman with such a warm character and to be sat listening to her wonderful anecdotes about her father is a memory I will always treasure. Sadly Mary passed away in 2018.

A sketch which is perhaps the earliest depiction of the South Pole Inn, where Mary grew up. The sketch featured in Tadhg Gahan's account *Polar Crean*.

Reproduced with permission from The Capuchin Annual (1952)

If you wish to discover more about the

man and the book, please visit:

www.tomcreanbook.com

Written In Memory Of Tom Crean

A Hero's Lament

Upon this frozen wasteland and pillowed snowy dunes

I dream of dear old Ireland And long to hear her tunes

The ripples of her rivers The voices hearts do yearn

Her misty mountain's whispering To these I must return

Yet onward I must travel As precious such is living

I ask you Lord please guide me through

This land of unforgiving

And grant to me a wish O Lord When duty I am done

Sail safely home to Erin green

An ever loving son

TIM FOLEY

REFERENCES

Preface

1. Joyce, P. W. 1875. *The Origin and History of Irish Names of Places (Second Series)*, M Glashan & Gill, 50 Upper Sackville St, Dublin, Whittaker & Co, Simpkin Marshall & Co, London, John Menzies, Edinburgh

Chapter 1 - The Road That Led South

1. Harkness. D. A. E. 1931. Irish Emigration, In: *Wilcox, Walter F., ed. International Migrations, Volume II: Interpretations*. NBER Volume. Cambridge, Massachusetts, ISBN: 0-87014-015-5, pp. 272-273

2. Irish Newspaper Archives, NA, *Kerry Sentinel*, April, 1880

3. Workhouses (Ireland) (Inmates), 6th March 1883, *Return of Inmates Workhouses* (Ireland). Printed by Henry Hansard and Son, London, Printers to the House of Commons

4. Irish Newspaper Archives, NA, *Kerry Sentinel*, August, 1886

5. O'Keeffe, Maurice and Jane. Oral Historians, *Irish Life and Lore*, CDDR01-05

6. The National Archives (TNA), *ADM/188*

7. BMH.WS1413.pdf, *Military Archives, Ireland*. p.17

8. https://api.parliament.uk/historic-hansard/written-answers/1916/nov/23/royal-navy-oath-of-allegiance

9. Crane, C. P. 1907. *Kerry*. Methuen & Co, 36 Essex St, London, p.200

10. The National Archives (TNA), *ADM/188/287/174699*

11. My Kerry Ancestors/Blog, *Tracing Tom Crean's Ancestors*, October 2014

12. The National Archives (TNA), *ADM/188/143/114127*

13. O'Keeffe, Maurice and Jane. Oral Historians, *Irish Life and Lore*, CDTP01-23

14. Hansard Committee Deb *Vol 19 cc1609-10* 18 December 1893 (Number of boys on Ship)

15. Hansard Committee Deb *Vol 21 cc595-6* 16 February 1894

16. Cowling, Henry. 1902. *From Lower Deck To Pulpit*. Partridge & Co. 8 and 9 Paternoster Row, London, (Life aboard a navy training ship)

17. *Ibid*

18. BMH.WS1413.pdf, *Military Archives*, Ireland. p.14

19. Skinner, George and Valerie. 2017. *The Life and Adventures of William Lashly, Vol 2.*

20. *British Colonist*, 21st May 1895 (Naval force at Corinto)

21. Irish Newspaper Archives, NA, May 1st 1895, *Belfast Newsletter* (USA Refuses to support Nicaragua)

22. Irish Newspaper Archive, *Leinster Express*, June 22nd 1895 (Death of Captain Trench)

23. The National Archives (TNA), *ADM/188/268/165484*

24. Yelverton, David. E. 2000. *Antarctica Unveiled*. University Press of Colorado, 5589 Arapahoe Avenue, Suite 206C, Boulder, CO 80303. p.92

25. The National Archives (TNA), *ADM/188/268/165484*

26. *Ibid*

27. Fatality Aboard The *Discovery*. (1902, January 3rd). *The Mercury* (Hobart, Tas: 1860-1954), p.2. http://nla.gov.au/ nla.news-article9577210 (Bonner funeral)

28. *Ibid*

29. Guly, H. R. 2012. 'Polar anaemia': cardiac failure during the heroic age of Antarctic exploration. *The Polar Record*, 48(2), 157–164. http://doi.org/10.1017/S0032247411000222

30. Guardian Newspaper Archive, *The Guardian*, September 12th 1904 (Death of Vince and Hare's return)

31. *Ibid*

32. Guardian Newspaper Archive, *The Guardian*, August 17th 1904 (Morning and Terra Nova helping to free Discovery)

33. Baughman, T. H. 1999. *Pilgrims on the Ice: Robert Falcon Scott's First Antarctic Expedition.* University of Nebraska Press, Lincoln and London, p.250 (Crean falls into ice and is rescued)

34. Guardian Newspaper Archive, *The Guardian*, September 14th 1904 (Scott and crew at Portsmouth)

35. Guardian Newspaper Archive, *The Guardian*, November 8th 1904 (Officers and crew at Royal Albert Hall to collect their medals)

36. RGS/CRM/43/ 1904, *List of Antarctic Medallists of the Royal Geographical Society by The President* (Sir Clements Markham). p.21

37. RGS/CRM/72/ 1905, *Antarctic Biographical Dictionary* by Sir Clements Markham

38. RGS/AA/3/1/22 1904, *Record of the R.G.S. Antarctic Silver Medallists*, quote by Sir Clements Markham).

39. Wilson, Christopher J, *http://www.antarcticbookshop.com/ acw.htm*

40. New Polar Voyage (1906, May 24th). *Evening Star (Boulder, WA: 1898-1921)*, p.2 (Second Edition). http://nla.gov.au/ nla.news-article204553903 (Lieutenant Barne's plans to go to Antarctica, 1906)

41. Ireland Civil Registration Indexes, 1845-1958. Database. *FamilySearch*. http://FamilySearch.org Accessed 2018. 4537923.pdf General Register Office, General Registry, Custom House, Dublin

42. The Late Capt. Scott. (1913, March 29th). *Queensland Times* (Ipswich, Qld.: 1909-1954), p.10 (Daily). http://nla.gov.au/nla.news-article113098853

Chapter 2 - Tom The Jumper

1. Yelverton, David. E. 2000. *Antarctica Unveiled*. University Press of Colorado, 5589 Arapahoe Avenue, Suite 206C, Boulder, CO 80303. p.180

2. Manchester Geographical Society, 1913, *The Journal of the Manchester Geographical Society*, Sherratt & Hughes, London and Manchester (Evans' speech)

3. Cherry-Garrard, A. 1922. *The Worst Journey in the World, Antarctic 1910-1913, Volumes One and Two*, George H. Doran Company, New York, Constable & Company Ltd., London

Chapter 3 - Tom The Walker

1. Manchester Geographical Society, 1913, *The Journal of the Manchester Geographical Society*, Sherratt & Hughes, London and Manchester (Evans' speech)

2. Debenham, F. *Tom Crean: An Appreciation*. Polar Record, 3 (17), 78-79. doi:10.1017/S0032247400038523, 1939

3. The Norwegian With Scott, Tryggve Gran's Antarctic Diary 1910-1913. Translated by Ellen Johanne McGhie (née Gran), 1984, London, National Maritime Museum, pp 216

4. From Polar Regions (1913, February 10th). Maitland Daily Mercury (Brisbane, Qld.: 1894-1939), p.5. http://nla.gov.au/nla.news-article121308647 (Scott is assumed safe)

5. Guardian Newspaper Archive, *The Guardian*, February 15th 1913 (Scott Memorial Service)

6. St. Paul's: a suggestion. (1913, February 15th). *The Daily Telegraph* (Sydney, NSW: 1883-1930), p.14. http://nla.gov.au/nla.news-article238621819

7. Captain Scott's "Good-Bye." (1913, June 23rd). *Advertiser (Adelaide, SA: 1889-1931)*, p.11(2). http://nla.gov.au/nla.news-article4416244 (Evans' lecture at Royal Albert Hall, May 21st 1913)

8. Guardian Newspaper Archive, *The Guardian*, November 1st 1913 (Evans at Manchester Free Trade Hall)

9. Terra Nova returns to Cardiff, (1913, August 13), Daily Standard (Brisbane, Qld. : 1912 - 1936), http://nla.gov.au/nla.news-article178875087

10. Ibid

11. Guardian Newspaper Archive, The Observer (London, Greater London, England), 20 Apr 1913

12. Terra Nova returns to Cardiff, (1913, August 13), Daily Standard (Brisbane, Qld. : 1912 - 1936), http://nla.gov.au/nla.news-article178875087

13. Ibid

14. Ibid

15. Guardian Newspaper Archive, *The Manchester Guardian*, October 29th 1921

16. Skinner, George and Valerie. 2017. *The Life and Adventures of William Lashly, second edition.* Privately published

17. Evans, Edward R.G.R, 1922, *South With Scott*, Collins Clear Type Press, London and Glasgow

18. Ellis, A. R. Lieut-Commander, 1969, *Under Scott's Command, Lashly's Antarctic Diaries*, R N, Taplinger Publishing Co. New York

Chapter 4 - Tom The Sailor

1. Guardian Newspaper Archive, *The Guardian*, December 29th 1914, (Announcement of Transantarctic Expedition)

2. *Ibid*

3. *Ibid*

4. Guardian Newspaper Archive, *The Manchester Guardian*, January 1st 1914 (Shackleton expresses doubt on use of aeroplanes)

5. Guardian Newspaper Archive, *The Guardian*, February 6th 1914 (Shackleton formally announces Captain as John King Davis)

6. Newspaper Archive, June 23rd 1914, *Sydney Morning Herald* (Frank Worsley formally announced as Captain of Endurance)

7. The Icy South (1914, May 4th), *Warwick Examiner and Times (Qld.: 1867-1919)*, p.3. http://nla.gov.au/nla.news-article82174128 (Crean wanted as boatswain by Foster Stackhouse)

8. Guardian Newspaper Archive, *The Guardian*, October 23rd 1913 (Foster Stackhouse announces British Antarctic Expedition)

9. Best Explorers (1914, January), *Darling Downs Gazzette (Qld.: 1881-1922)*, p.7. http://nla.gov.au/nla.news-article196878153 (Foster Stackhouse singles out Crean for praise)

10. Guardian Newspaper Archive, *The Guardian*, June 23rd 1914 (Foster Stackhouse announces '7-year-cruise')

11. Irish Newspaper Archives, NA, *The Irish Examiner*, June 23rd 1914 (Crean announced for inclusion of Endurance expedition)

12. Has Shackleton failed? (1916, March 25th), *The Argus (Melbourne, Vic.: 1848-1957)*, p.18. http://nla.gov.au/ nla.news-article2106337 (Reference to Crean being part of the crossing party)

13. Guardian Newspaper Archives, *The Guardian*, NA, December 30th 1913 (Shackleton details plans for Endurance expedition and confirmed talks with Stackhouse - No rivalry or crossover of the missions)

14. Hoehling, A. A. and Hoehling, M. D. 1996. *The Last Voyage of the Lusitania*. Lanham, MD; Madison Books, p.149

15. The National Archives (TNA), *ADM/188/287/174699*

16. https://winstonchurchill.hillsdale.edu/churchill-and-the-hms-enchantress/

17. *Ibid*

18. Guardian Newspaper Archive, *The Manchester Guardian*, July 17th 1914 (Queen visits Endurance)

19. Guardian Newspaper Archives, *The Guardian*, NA, July 15th 1914 (Confirmation of three boats and a motor launch on Endurance)

20. Guardian Newspaper Archives, *The Guardian*, NA, August 3rd 1914

21. *Ibid*

22. *Ibid*

23. Thomson, John. 2003. *Elephant Island and beyond: the life and diaries of Thomas Orde Lees*, Bluntisham Books, Erskine Press, Norwich

24. Guardian Newspaper Archive, *The Guardian*, March 27th 1916 (Recollection of Crean while deliberating on what has happened to Shackleton and the Endurance crew)

25. Irish Newspaper Archives, NA, *Irish Examiner*, 2nd January, 1920 (Gloating over pebbles like misers over gold)

26. Guardian Newspaper Archives, *The Guardian*, NA, November 9th 1916 (Wild describing how Crean saved the James Caird at the launch)

Chapter 5 - Tom The Climber

1. Gilkes, Michael, *"It ain't necessarily so": South Georgia Loose Ends*. Accessed February 2018 website.lineone.net/~polar.publishing/southgeorgialooseends.htm

2. Robertson, R. B. 1961. *Of Whales And Men*. Alfred A. Knopf, New York

3. https://www.naval-history.net/*OWShips-WW1-08-HMS_Avoca.htm*

4. https://www.rmg.co.uk/discover/behind-the-scenes/blog/fine-copy-diary-kept-gw-smith-steward-onboard-rms-vessel-avon

5. https://www.fig.gov.fk/archives/jdownloads/The%20Falkland%20Islands%20Magazine/FIM%201916%20May-Aug.pdf (Shackleton speech in Falkland Islands June 3rd 1916)

6. https://www.gov.uk/government/uploads/system/uploads/attachment_data/file/550934/ Pardo_and_Shackleton_Article UKAHT Antarctic_Times.pdf

7. Irish Newspaper Archives, NA, *Irish Independent*, September 5th 1916

8. Shackleton, Ernest. 1920. *South: The Story of Shackleton's Last Expedition 1914 - 1917*. The Macmillan Company, New York, p.211

9. Guardian Newspaper Archive, *The Manchester Guardian*, November 8th 1916 (Frank Wild interview)

10. Guardian Newspaper Archive, *The Observer*, November 26th 1916 (Frank Wild interview describing a typical day)

11. Guardian Newspaper Archive, *The Observer*, December 19th 1916 (George Marston - From nowhere to London)

12. Mill, Hugh Robert. 1923. *The Life of Sir Ernest Shackleton, C.V.O., O.B.E.* (Mil.), LL.D. W. Heinemann, London. pp. 265-266 (Lectures at Philharmonic)

13. Irish Newspaper Archives, NA, *Irish Independent*, February 26th 1920 (Crean on stage for Shackleton's 100th lecture)

14. Irish Newspaper Archives, NA, *Irish Independent,* August 4th 1916

Chapter 6 - Tom - Post Antarctica

1. Smith, Gordon. Naval History (.net), */OWShips-WW1-05-HMS_ King_Alfred.htm* (Crean leaves HMS King Alfred)

2. Irish Newspaper Archives, NA, *Southern Star, November 7th 1998*

3. Irish Newspaper Archives, NA, September 28th 1957, *The Kerryman* (Oates riding at Ballyvelly races)

4. Irish Newspaper Archives, NA, *Southern Star,* November 7th 1998

5. Irish Newspaper Archives, NA, *Southern Star*, August 29th 1981

6. Irish Newspaper Archives, NA, *Kerry Evening Post*, March 17th 1917

7. Irish Newspaper Archives, NA, *The Liberator*, April 24th 1917

8. *The Navy List, London: Volume December 1918.* Her Majesty's Stationary Office, digitised by National Library of Scotland (Boatswain on Inflexible)

9. Nash, N. S. 2009. *K Boat Catastrophe: Eight Ships and Five Collisions - The Full Story of the 'Battle of the Isle of May'*, Pen & Sword Maritime, Barnsley, p.114

10. Personal copy of Captain's commendation certificate, available by request

11. Smith, Gordon. *Naval History (.net), / WW1z05NorthRussia.htm*

12. Smith, Gordon. *Naval History (.net), /OWShips-WW1-05-HMS_Fox.htm (HMS Fox Logs)*

13. *Ibid*

14. *Ibid*

15. Singleton-Gates, G. R. 1920. *Bolos and Barishynas, Gale and Polden Ltd.*, (Evacuation of HMS Fox September 27th 1919)

16. The National Archives (TNA), *ADM/196/157/554*

17. *Ibid*

18. Irish Newspaper Archives, NA, *Belfast Newsletter*, March 27th 1920 (Forde Shot)

19. Irish Newspaper Archives, NA, *The Killarney Echo*, April 17th 1920 (Tralee Protest)

20. Irish Newspaper Archives, NA, *The Irish Examiner*, April 26th 1920 (Wife of Cornelius Crean expressed her concern)

21. Irish Newspaper Archives, NA, *The Irish Examiner*, April 29th 1920 (Funeral of Cornelius Crean)

22. Irish Newspaper Archives, NA, *The Irish Independent*, October 7th 1920 (Case against two Annascaul men in Cork)

23. Irish Newspaper Archives, NA, *The Irish Examiner*, January 31st 1922 (Death of Shackleton)

24. Irish Newspaper Archives, NA, *The Irish Examiner*, February 1st 1922 (Shackleton's coffin and guard of honour)

25. Guardian Newspaper Archive, *The Manchester Guardian*, February 16th 1922 (Shackleton's coffin taken to South Georgia)

26. Irish Newspaper Archives, NA, *The Liberator*, January 3rd 1921 (P J O'Neill sentenced to 5 years)

27. Irish Newspaper Archive, *Kerry Reporter*, March 28th 1925 (Crean on Annascaul Coal Committee)

28. BMH.WS0960.pdf, *Military Archives*, Ireland. p.12

29. www.historyireland.com *18ᵗʰ-19ᵗʰ-Century History, 20ᵗʰ- century/Contemporary History, Features, Issue 2* (Summer 2003), Volume 11 (Crean's perceived support for DeValera)

30. Irish Newspaper Archives, NA, *Kerryman,* October 4ᵗʰ 1924 (Irish Pilgrimage to Lourdes)

31. Ireland Civil Registration Indexes, 1845-1958. Database. FamilySearch. http://FamilySearch.org Accessed 2018. 4374253.pdf General Register Office, General Registry, Custom House, Dublin

32. Ireland Civil Registration Indexes, 1845-1958. Database. FamilySearch. http://FamilySearch.org Accessed 2018. 4372559.pdf General Register Office, General Registry, Custom House, Dublin

33. Irish Newspaper Archives, NA, *The Liberator*, June 1ˢᵗ 1926 (Proposed sale of South Pole Inn 1926)

34. Irish Newspaper Archives, NA, *The Liberator*, December 24ᵗʰ 1927 (Proposed sale of South Pole Inn for January 1928)

35. Irish Newspaper Archives, NA, *The Liberator*, April 23ʳᵈ 1926 (Dan O'Sullivan visit)

36. O'Keeffe, Maurice and Jane. Oral Historians, *Irish Life and Lore*, CDTP01-23

37. Irish Newspaper Archives, NA, *Kerry Champion*, January 30ᵗʰ 1930 (Crean confirms house rebuilt in 1929)

38. O'Keeffe, Maurice and Jane. Oral Historians, *Irish Life and Lore*, CDTP01-23

39. Huxley, Elspeth. 1978. *Scott Of The Antarctic*. Atheneum, New York, p.275

40. Ireland Civil Registration Indexes, 1845-1958. Database. FamilySearch. http://FamilySearch.org Accessed 2018. 4319593.pdf General Register Office, General Registry, Custom House, Dublin

41. Irish News Archives, *Irish Examiner*, December 10th, 2000 (Crean's daughter revealed he loved boxing).

42. O'Keeffe, Maurice and Jane. Oral Historians, *Irish Life and Lore*, CDTP01-23

43. Irish Newspaper Archives, NA, *The Evening Herald* (Dublin), October 19th 1936 (Stealing the Trawler)

44. Irish Newspaper Archives, NA, *The Liberator*, June 20th 1936 (2hr chase of Girl Pat)

45. Irish Newspaper Archives, NA, *The Belfast Newsletter*, October 23rd 1936 (Orsborne's sentenced)

46. Irish Newspaper Archives, NA, *Irish Press*, October 24th 1936 (John Vincent volunteers to bring Girl Pat home)

47. O'Keeffe, Maurice and Jane. Oral Historians, *Irish Life and Lore*, CDTP01-23

48. Irish Newspaper Archives, NA, *The Liberator*, January 14th 1930 (Crean brings court case)

49. Irish Newspaper Archives, NA, *The Kerry Champion*, June 24th 1933 (Crean taken to court)

50. Personal copy of baptism certificate, available on request

Chapter 7 - Tom - The Final Journey

1. Irish Newspaper Archives, NA, *Southern Star*, April 23rd 1938 (Admiral's fishing holiday)

2. Irish Newspaper Archives, NA, *The Kerryman,* August 20th 1938 (Crean funeral and Evans tribute)

Chapter 8 - The Legacy And The Campaign

1. Irish Newspaper Archives, NA, *Irish Examiner,* June 5th 1949 (Robert Forde with Ellen Crean)

2. Irish Newspaper Archives, NA, *Connaught Tribune*, August 3rd 1957 (Donal O'Leary Irish Hero article)

3. Irish Newspaper Archives, NA, *Irish Independent*, December 30th 1955 (Tom Crean article)

4. Barry, Denis. 1952. *Polar Crean: The Capuchin Annual.* John English & Co, Ltd., Wexford

5. https://1916.rte.ie/relevant-places/fantastic-rumours-were-mixed-with-the-facts/

6. Irish Newspaper Archives, NA, *Westmeath Independent*, August 18th, 1928 (Dermot Barry, (Tadhg Gahan), wins literary prize)

7. Irish Newspaper Archives, NA, *Irish Independent*, October 10th, 1931 (Tom Creagan book published)

8. The National Archives (TNA), *ADM/196/34*

9. Irish Newspaper Archives, NA, *The Kerryman*, August 16th 1985 (Appeal for donations to purchase Tom Crean Letters to Lieut. J. P. Kennedy)

10. Irish Newspaper Archives, NA, *The Kerryman*, September 25th 1987 (Dingle Library Tom Crean Exhibition and Plaque at South Pole Inn - John Knightly there to celebrate his hero and godfather)

11. Irish Newspaper Archives, NA, *The Kerryman*, April 18th 1987 (Tralee Council consider honouring Crean by naming a town Square)

12. Irish Newspaper Archives, NA, *The Kerryman*, March 14th 1997 (Ryle Dwyer - Tom Crean still lacks deserved recognition)

13. Irish Newspaper Archives, NA, *The Kerryman*, April 11th 2002, (Edmund Hilary in Tralee to open exhibition)

14. Irish Newspaper Archives, NA, *The Kerryman*, July 24th 2003, (Crean statue unveiled in Annascaul)

Epilogue

1. The National Archives (TNA), *ADM/188/300/180517*

2.https://www.fig.gov.fk/archives/online-collections/people/ 19th-century-families/s-to-z (Daniel O'Sullivan lifesaving incident and Falkland Islands career overview)

3. The National Archives (TNA), *ADM/188/290/176129*

4. Irish Newspaper Archives, NA, *The Kerryman*, April 13th 1935 (Funeral of P. J.O'Neill)

Appendix - A Compilation Of Related Matter

1. Irish Newspaper Archives, NA, *Southern Star*, November 7th 1998 (Letters to Captain Dodds)

2. Irish Newspaper Archives, NA, *Southern Star*, February 11th 1913 (Interview with Scott before departure of Terra Nova)

3. Guardian Newspaper Archive, *The Guardian*, March 8th 1912 - (Interview with Scott before Terra Nova departed)

4. Images of letter - https://www.andrusierautographs.com/product/scott-robert-falcon-1868-1912/

5. Simpson, G.C. D Sc, F.R.S. 1919, *British Antarctic Expedition 1910-1913, Meteorology, Volume 1 Discussion, Prepared under the Directions of the Committee for the Publication of Scientific Results*, Printed by Thacker Spink and Co. Calcutta)

6. Solomon, Susan. Stearns, Charles R. November 1999, *On the role of the weather in the deaths of R. F. Scott and his companions 96 (23) 13012-13016*; DOI: 10.1073/pnas.96.23.13012. Proceedings of the National Academy of Sciences

7. Sienicki, Krzysztof. 2016, *Captain Scott: Icy Deceits and Untold Realities*, Open Academic Press. Berlin

Book Acknowledgements

Amitage, Albert. 1905. *Two Years in the Antarctic*. Edward Arnold, London, 41 & 43 Maddox St, Bond St W

Arranged by Huxley, Leonard. 1914. *Scott's Last Expedition, In Two Volumes*. Smith, Elder & Co, 15 Waterloo Place, London

Baughman, T. H. 1999. *Pilgrims On The Ice: Robert Falcon Scott's First Expedition*. University of Nevada Press, Lincoln and London

Cherry-Garrard, Apsley. 1922. *The Worst Journey in the World, In Two Volumes, Volume One & Volume Two*. George H. Doran Company, New York, Constable & Company Ltd., London

Debenham, F. 1939. *Tom Crean: An Appreciation*. Polar Record, 3(17), 78-79. doi:10.1017/S0032247400038523

Ellis, A. R., Lieut-Commander. 1969. *Under Scott's Command, Lashly's Antarctic Diaries*. R. N. Taplinger Publishing Co., Inc.

Evans, Edward R. G. R. 1922. *South With Scott*. Collins Clear Type Press, London and Glasgow

Griffith Taylor, Thomas. 1916. *With Scott: The Silver Lining*. Smith, Elder & Co, 15 Waterloo Place, London

Hoehling, A. A. and Hoehling, M. D. 1996. *The Last Voyage of the Lusitania*. Lanham, MD; Madison Books

Huxley, Elspeth. 1978. *Scott Of The Antarctic*. Atheneum, New York Mill

Hugh Robert. 1923. *The Life of Sir Ernest Shackleton*, C.V.O., O.B.E. (Mil.), LL.D. W. Heinemann, London.

McGhie (née Gran), Ellen Johanne,1984. *Translation of The Norwegian With Scott, Tryggve Gran's Antarctic Diary 1910-1913*. National Maritime Museum, Her Majesty's Stationary Office, London.

Robertson, R. B. 1961. *Of Whales And Men*. Alfred A. Knopf, New York

Shackleton, Ernest. 1920. *South: The Story of Shackleton's Last Expedition 1914 - 1917*. The Macmillan Company, New York

Singleton-Gates, G. R. 1920. *Bolos and Barishynas*. Gale and Polden Ltd.

Smith, Michael. 2000. *An Unsung Hero - Tom Crean - Antarctic Survivor*. The Collins Press, Cork

Spufford, Francis. 1997. *I May Be Some Time: Ice and the English Imagination*. St Martin's Press, New York

Wilson, Edward Adrian. 1972. *Diary of the Terra Nova Expedition to the Antarctic, 1910-1912*. Editor, H. G. R. King, Humanities Press

Worsley, Frank Arthur. 1977. *Shackleton's Boat Journey*. WW Norton & Company, Inc.

Yelverton, David. E. 2000. *Antarctica Unveiled*. University Press of Colorado, 5589 Arapahoe Avenue, Suite 206C, Boulder, CO 80303.

INDEX

250

The Campaign on Social Media

Ireland Should Honour Tom Crean on Facebook

Ireland Should Honour Tom Crean on Twitter

Ireland Should Honour Tom Crean on Instagram

The Book on Social Media

Crean The Extraordinary Life of an Irish Hero on Facebook

Crean The Extraordinary Life of an Irish Hero on Twitter

Crean The Extraordinary Life of an Irish Hero on Instagram

The Petition

Tom Crean Petition on Change